Advance Praise for *The Founder Within*

'A practical guide for transforming you into a founder who thinks clearly, acts decisively and stays resilient under pressure, enabling you to build an enterprise that doesn't just grow but survives, adapts and lasts.'

Sandeep Das
Storytelling coach and bestselling author

'Indraveer Singh brilliantly shifts the focus from surface-level growth hacks to the "inner architecture" of a founder, showing that a startup cannot truly mature if its leader doesn't. *The Founder Within* is an essential thinking companion for anyone looking to build something that works, matters and lasts.'

Harsh Pamnani
Bestselling author of *Booming Brands*, *Booming Digital Stars* and *From Unknown to Unforgettable*

'*The Founder Within* shall definitely inspire readers to discover that the real venture is not just a company but consciousness; not just growth but growth with grace; not just ambition but ambition aligned with higher purpose. May this work empower many to lead with integrity, resilience and compassion, and to recognise that the most powerful enterprise one can build is the awakened self.'

Rohan Tandon
Director, Restaurant Technology, McDonald's, USA

'*The Founder Within* offers a refreshing perspective on entrepreneurship by shifting attention from startup hype to the mindset and discipline of the founder. What I found especially valuable is its emphasis on the inner journey that shapes real business decisions, resilience and growth. Indraveer Singh brings together practical insight and thoughtful reflection in a way that will resonate with both aspiring and practising founders. This is a meaningful and relevant book for anyone wanting to build not only a venture but also the clarity and character required to sustain it.'

Dr Himanshu Sharma
Lecturer, Auckland University of Technology, New Zealand

'In an ecosystem often obsessed with funding, valuation and speed, *The Founder Within* brings the focus back to the first principle – the founder's mindset. Indraveer goes beyond startup mechanics to examine mindset, discipline and decision frameworks that define long-term success in any entrepreneurial journey. This book does not glorify entrepreneurship; it humanises it. It is not a playbook of shortcuts; it is a framework for building founders who can build institutions. A must-read and long-term companion for early-stage founders, student entrepreneurs and professionals transitioning into leadership!'

Rohit Singh
Former scientist at ISRO; Assistant director, IN-SPACe

THE FOUNDER WITHIN

THE FOUNDER WITHIN

How Top 1% Entrepreneurs Think, Decide and Build Enduring Ventures

INDRAVEER SINGH

Foreword by K. Ganesh

BLOOMSBURY
NEW DELHI • LONDON • OXFORD • NEW YORK • SYDNEY

BLOOMSBURY INDIA
Bloomsbury Publishing India Pvt. Ltd
Second Floor, LSC Building No. 4, DDA Complex, Pocket C – 6 & 7,
Vasant Kunj, New Delhi, 110070

BLOOMSBURY, BLOOMSBURY INDIA and the Diana logo are
trademarks of Bloomsbury Publishing Plc

First published in India 2026

ISBN: HB: 978-93-69527-52-6; PB: 978-93-69528-08-0;
eBook: 978-93-69520-35-0

2 4 6 8 10 9 7 5 3 1

Typeset in Bembo by Manipal Technologies Limited
Printed and bound in India by Thomson Press India Private Limited

MIX
Paper | Supporting responsible forestry
FSC® C010615

To find out more about our authors and books visit www.bloomsbury.com and sign up for our newsletters

To my Spiritual Master,
who personifies resilience,
clarity and undeterred cause

Contents

Foreword

IN 1990, I STARTED my first company with ₹84,000 and a business card that essentially said 'computer mechanic'. There were no venture capitalists (VCs) in India, no angel investors, no accelerators, no startup podcasts telling me I needed a morning routine involving cold showers and gratitude journals. There was just a problem that I had spotted at HCL – there were companies with computers from twelve different vendors and nobody to fix them – and a somewhat bold belief that I could build a business around it. I had no playbook, no mentor, no framework. I just took a leap.

Over the next three decades, I would go on to start several more companies, sell a few, shut one down, watch a few grow into things I couldn't have imagined and learn more from the failures than from the wins. Along the way, Meena and I have worked alongside dozens of founders, through late nights and cash crunches and moments when everything seemed to have nearly fallen apart. And if there is one learning I have taken away from all of it, it is this: the company always ends up looking like the founder. Always. For better or for worse.

When the product breaks, you can fix the product. When the market shifts, you can pivot. When you run out of money, you can, if you're resourceful enough, find more money. But when the founder's thinking is off, when the internal wiring is faulty, everything downstream starts to wobble. I have watched brilliant ideas die because the person behind them couldn't handle conflict in the team, or couldn't let go of control at the right time, or treated cash like it was somebody else's problem. None of these are business failures. They are personal ones. And they are the ones nobody prepares you for.

That is why when Indraveer shared *The Founder Within* with me, I found myself nodding through it in a way I rarely do with books about startups. Most of them obsess over mechanics: how to raise a round, how to hack growth, how to build a pitch deck that will make investors salivate. All useful, sure. But they skip the part that actually determines whether any of it works. The founder. The person. The mess of fears, biases, blind spots, and stubbornness that enters the room every morning and makes a hundred decisions before lunch.

Indraveer doesn't skip that part. He goes straight at it.

And he does it at exactly the right time. There has never been a better moment to start a company in India. AI has compressed what used to take a team of twenty into something a founder with a laptop alone can pull off in a weekend. The digital public infrastructure, UPI, Aadhaar, ONDC (Open Network for Digital Commerce) have lowered the barriers to starting up in ways that were unprecedented anywhere in the world. The cost of experimentation has collapsed. The market is over a billion people with smartphones and growing purchasing power. If you are sitting on an idea and waiting for some cosmic green signal, this is it.

But here is what worries me. I spend a lot of time around young, talented, ambitious people, and a shocking number of them are still on the fence. Researching instead of building. Waiting for the perfect co-founder, the perfect idea, the perfect market timing. Perfection, as any founder will tell you, is just procrastination wearing a nice suit. The infrastructure is ready. The tools are ready. The only question is whether you are, and that has everything to do with what's going on inside your head.

That's the territory this book walks into. With honesty, without TED talk energy, without promoting hustle porn, without pretending that entrepreneurship is some glamorous adventure where everything works out if you just believe hard enough. It is messy. It is lonely. Some days you go from feeling euphoria to complete hopelessness before noon. The founders who make it through are the ones who have done the inner work, who know themselves well enough to make good decisions under pressure, who can tell the difference between conviction and stubbornness.

Read this slowly. Argue with it. Underline the bits that sting. And then go build something. The world is not short of problems worth solving. What it is short of are founders who have done the work on themselves before asking the world to believe in their vision. This book is a very good place to start that work.

K. Ganesh
Serial entrepreneur; Co-founder, GrowthStory.in;
Promoter, BigBasket, BlueStone and more

Introduction

Building a startup is tough. Building the founder behind it is tougher. 'Founder' – a badge that now sells dreams faster than products. It sits proudly in Instagram bios, sparkles in LinkedIn posts, and shows up at college startup fests with hoodies and hashtags. All echoing: 'Building something of my own.' For some, it embodies rebellion; for others, ambition, or an ultimate escape from the 9-to-5 lifestyle.

The truth is, none of this makes you a founder. Building something that works, that matters, and that lasts – that's the real initiation. This book is not extolling founders or startups. It's an honest exploration of whether entrepreneurship fits someone and, if it does, how one evolves as a founder while the startup evolves. It exposes the vanity and illusion often attached with the coveted 'founder' title, replacing it with clarity, depth and entrepreneurial awareness.

Maybe you're a college student whose notebook is full of startup sketches, ideas and late-night 'what ifs'. Maybe you're a professional sitting in a corporate job, quietly questioning whether your skills are building your dream or someone else's. Maybe you're a founder in motion – building a product, managing chaos, doubt and deadlines, and learning the hard way that 'being your own boss' isn't the freedom it's marketed to be; or maybe you're a business leader who has already built something but is trying to think like a founder again, to bring agility back to their decisions, seeking a compass to progress with clarity.

The startup world doesn't care about your GPA, your résumé, your hierarchical seniority in a multinational corporation, or how 'disruptive' your pitch sounds at an open mic. It cares about how you think when the pressure hits and decisions matter more than your default actions. It rewards your ability to adapt when everything changes overnight. It tests whether you can keep moving when nothing is working and everyone, including you, is questioning your sanity and sensibility behind hustling for a dream.

If startups were only about ideas, every college dorm room would be a breeding ground for unicorns. But here's what really separates the ones who make it from the ones who fade away: their mindset.

Behind every real venture lies something far less glamorous. Long nights, silent failures, awkward self-discovery and a founder's inner evolution that rarely gets announced on stage. Beyond all the show and vanity, entrepreneurship tests your endurance, clarity and character that few titled 'founders' anticipate until they're already in it. Being a founder is about learning to navigate uncertainty with courage, failure with dignity, and growth with sharp cognisance. It's about discovering what truly drives you when no one's watching, and the spotlight fades.

As popularly said, building a startup is like building a plane mid-air while the blueprint is still downloading, and you're also the pilot, engineer and cabin crew.

Take Melanie Perkins, the co-founder of Canva. While she was in college, she would also tutor design students, which made her realise how painfully complex design tools were. Her idea was simple – make design accessible to everyone rather than have learners and professionals rely on expensive licensed software. What followed was a masterclass in founder grit. Over a hundred investors said 'No'. She didn't pivot to something trendier. Instead, she refined her conviction. It took years before someone finally said 'Yes'.

Canva didn't explode overnight. It grew through patience, clarity and relentless simplification. So Melanie built persistence within before building a product. And that humble, focused and problem-driven mindset turned her classroom frustration into a global platform empowering millions.[1]

Every founder's journey is proof that when one untaps the entrepreneurial traits within, everything else follows. It's the inner architecture that turns chaotic beginnings into success beyond imagination.

Vidit Aatrey, co-founder of Meesho, didn't begin with millions or a Silicon Valley address. He began with a WhatsApp group and an idea to empower small-town sellers in Bharat to start businesses from their phones. He and his team spent years listening to real sellers, experimenting with broken models, and surviving on belief when logic ran out.[2]

Whether you look at Melanie or Vidit, their real edge wasn't technology. It was stubborn grit and the willingness to unlearn, adapt and stay real. That mindset, not money, transformed a simple reselling app into one of India's fastest-growing startups. What connects Canva and Meesho isn't geography, industry or funding. It's mindset – the ability to keep building when the world keeps doubting. That's what makes a founder. Founders live at the intersection of chaos and conviction, and are expected to be visionary and grounded, brave yet thoughtful, fast but not reckless.

No startup outgrows its founder. As the venture evolves, so must the vision, the team and, most importantly, the person steering it. The startup's next level always demands a better version of the founder. One who learns faster, listens more deeply and leads more wisely.

And that's why this book exists – to talk about *that* side of entrepreneurship. It traces a founder's inner journey that happens alongside the startup's outer journey.

Entrepreneurship is about qualitatively calibrating yourself as a founder from within. And thus, *The Founder Within* isn't just another book about startups. It's a book about self-discovery through creation. The evolution of a founder who grows as the startup grows.

Why This Book Exists

Clearly, this isn't another 'how-to' manual on raising capital or hacking first million users or building from zero. Every 'startup guru' webinar or YouTube playlist titled '10 Growth Hacks That Changed My Life' is shouting this all to you.

This book is about something far more foundational, i.e., learning to think, act and evolve like a founder from the inside out. Because every business problem begins as a founder's problem. Every pivot, partnership and product is triggered by an internal shift long before it becomes an external move. A startup cannot mature if its founder doesn't.

The Founder Within doesn't exalt entrepreneurship. It humanises it. It's not written for the 'wannabe disruptor' chasing buzzwords, but for those quietly building, breaking and learning. It's for the students dreaming beyond classrooms, the professionals transitioning from jobs to journeys, and the founders figuring it out in real time. Rather than giving formulas or tactics, this book helps you ask the right questions and shows you how to do it right.

The Real Game Is Inner, Not Outer

Startup education today obsesses over surface-level mechanics such as fundraising, scaling, product–market fit, growth hacks, etc. All useful. But none of it works if the steering founder behind it is shaky in actions and decisions.

You can copy another company's product, but not its founder's entrepreneurial character. Thus, a founder is a startup's core differentiating competence and unique selling point (USP). Startups collapse when founders lose internal alignment among their purpose, people and priorities. And that misalignment almost always begins unobtrusively, inside the founder's own head.

A founder's entrepreneurial smartness, mental tenacity and balanced decision-making are what sail through chaos and confusion. But the truth is, no MBA programme can prepare a founder to reach this stage of maturity overnight. Rather, it's a gradual inner evolution of a founder. And thus, the journey of building a startup makes a founder move through several mindset shifts.

That's why this book focuses on mindset evolution – how you, as a founder, can transform across phases. The early stage demands clarity and courage. The growth stage demands focus and discipline. The scaling stage demands agility and systems thinking. Each phase requires a different version of you. And *The Founder Within* helps you uncover that version, one mindset at a time.

By the time you finish this book, I hope that you'll have clarity on:

- How to build the inner strength, focus and conviction that every founder needs before funding or fame ever arrives.
- How to manage risk, fear and uncertainty with courage and clarity and move from procrastination to action.
- How to attract, build and lead high-trust teams that grow with you, not away from you.
- How to handle money, equity and capital without losing control, clarity or character.
- How to measure real traction, adapt when things break, and scale with systems that last.
- How to evolve as a founder – from first idea to final exit – while staying grounded, self-aware and purpose-driven through it all.

As mentioned earlier, this book is surely not a manual. It's a mental gym. More than hype, it's about inner calibration. It's the navigation for those who'd rather build something real than chase every shiny trend. If you've ever felt that tug in your gut, that restlessness to create, to lead, to try, then welcome. This isn't about starting up. It's about starting within.

Each chapter dissects one key founder mindset – from courage and focus to capital clarity and scalability. It's not the theory. It's the reflection into inevitable scenarios. It won't glorify the grind. It will humanise the process. It's meant to make you pause, think, and reset how you approach to growth, leadership and self-mastery as a founder.

It's a book about *you*. Entrepreneurship just happens to be the mirror that reveals who you really are – your fears, biases, resilience and blind spots. When you lead people, you discover patience. When you manage chaos, you uncover focus. When you fail, you learn detachment. When you win, you confront ego.

How Is This Book Built?

Startups have playbooks. Founders rarely do. This book aims to change that. It's crafted as a thinking companion to slow you down at every major milestone just enough to think sharper, see clearer and act wiser.

After all, entrepreneurship isn't a reckless ride; it's a series of conscious resets. And every reset starts in the founder's mind and choices. *The Founder Within* is structured like a mirror – divided into 16 distinct mindsets, each reflecting a critical stage of a founder's evolution. As your startup grows through its messy, magical phases from idea to traction to scale, this book travels with you through an evolving and maturing mindset. The chapters track that inner growth.

Each mindset and each chapter is built around four anchors:

1. **The Core Principle:** What this mindset really means and why it matters.
2. **The Real Story:** Several cases or anecdotes from real founders who lived it.
3. **The Practice:** How to apply it through choices, decisions or reflections.
4. **The Shift:** The inner rewiring that this mindset triggers once understood.

The book's three arcs mirror the founder's natural trajectory of growth as an entrepreneur.

Arc One: Building the Inner Core focuses on the courage, clarity, focus and execution infrastructure you need before capital or traction arrive.

Arc Two: Capital, Clarity and Control extends into the realities of team-building, equity, money and storytelling, where the founder must balance the heart with structure.

Arc Three: Growth, Grit and Goodbye explores the stages of maturity from traction and scale to pivots and exits that turn leadership into legacy.

You can read this book in sequence or jump to whichever mindset you're currently battling. Some readers start at 'The Execution Mindset' when they're overwhelmed by tasks. Others go straight to 'The Team Mindset' when people's problems dominate. There's no wrong way to read it, only an honest one.

Every chapter carries short reflection prompts as 'Mindset Cues'. These aren't prescriptive, but they're planted to encourage inner work. Treat them as your 'pause moments'. They help you look into your own decision-making patterns and overall cognition. Because growth doesn't start when you read something new. It starts when you confront something true.

Think of this book as a travel journal. Something to return to after every crash, pivot or milestone. So read slowly. Question deeply. Highlight what clicks strongly because the most important startup you'll ever build is the one inside you. You don't need funding papers or a pitch deck to start thinking like a founder. You need ownership of your vision, your decisions and your actions.

As said before, this book won't give you any shortcuts. It'll give you the truth. It won't make things easier. It'll make them clearer instead.

This book is written to provide practical insights and a grounded understanding of the entrepreneurial journey. In addition to the author's experience and perspectives, the content is supported by research drawn from credible media articles, research studies, founders' podcasts and interviews to enhance its depth and reliability. Every effort has been made to ensure accuracy and relevance for both aspiring and experienced entrepreneurs. Readers are encouraged to share feedback or point out any inaccuracies to help improve future editions.

So, let's begin with the idea of identity, from doing to becoming. Let's awaken the founder within.

Arc 1

Building the Inner Core

1

The Foundation Mindset

The Get-Set Point

Entrepreneurship isn't a calm stroll in the park; it's more like riding a roller coaster with zero seat belts while juggling flaming torches. It's thrilling, unpredictable and downright exhausting. But at the heart of every startup that rises above the chaos isn't just a brilliant idea or a fat bank account. It's something far more powerful – the founder's mindset.

Think of the founder's mindset as your startup's secret sauce. It's the invisible force behind every decision, every sleepless night, and every 'let's pivot' moment. It shapes how you react when your carefully crafted plans hit a wall, how you inspire your team when the going gets tough, and how you keep your eyes on the prize even when the market feels like shifting sands.

Here's the kicker: startups don't usually fail because their ideas are poor. Nope. They fail because founders get stuck in the maze of 'what ifs', paralysed by uncertainty, distracted by shiny trends, or burnt out by relentless pressure. The founder's mindset is what helps you slice through that maze with resilience, clarity and a dash of guts.

Entrepreneurs are often labelled as dreamers – starry-eyed folks chasing unicorns. But here's the truth: their minds work like nimble acrobats. They're not just staring at obstacles; they're scanning the horizon for opportunities hidden in plain sight. This mindset is all about cognitive flexibility – the ability to flip your thinking, shake off setbacks, and rewrite the rules as you go.

Ever heard of Carol Dweck's 'Growth Mindset'? It's the idea that your capabilities aren't engraved on stone; they're like muscles you can train with effort and grit. Successful founders embody this mindset. They see failure not as a full stop but as a comma – a chance to tweak, learn and leap forward with better moves.

But here's the thing: balancing a clear vision with wild adaptability isn't something you're born with. It's forged in the fire of experience, mistakes and relentless self-reflection.

The Four Superpowers That Founders Leverage

After years of working with startups and diving into founder stories, I've distilled the founder's mindset to four core traits. Master these, and you're already playing in the big leagues.

Resilience: Turning Setbacks into Superpowers

Picture this: your pitch gets rejected for the fifth time this week, your prototype breaks, and your cash runway looks more like a puddle. The universe seems determined to test you. But resilience? That's what turns you into an entrepreneurial ninja.

Resilience isn't just about bouncing back. It's about bouncing forward. It's the power to learn from every crash, rebuild smarter, and keep hustling even when it feels like the world's against you.

When it comes to resilience, one inspiring story is that of Sara Blakely, the founder of Spanx. Sara started her business journey with just $5,000 in savings and no formal business training. She faced repeated rejections – from manufacturers who doubted her product to department stores that were hesitant to stock her innovative shapewear. Rather than giving up, Sara used each rejection as fuel to refine her pitch, improve her product, and explore new opportunities. She famously tested her prototype on herself, cutting the feet off control-top pantyhose to create her first Spanx product. Sara's relentless persistence paid off when Oprah Winfrey endorsed Spanx on her show, catapulting the brand into the spotlight. Today, Sara Blakely is a self-made billionaire, a testament to how resilience and a refusal to quit can turn humble beginnings into extraordinary success.[1]

Want to build resilience? Surround yourself with people who uplift you, break big goals into bite-sized wins, and treat every failure like a free MBA in 'What Not to Do'.

Decisiveness: Choosing to Act (Even When It's Messy)

The startup world is messy, noisy, and often doesn't hand you all the facts on a silver platter. Waiting for perfect info? That's a sure way to miss the train. Decisive founders know when to trust their gut and act, even when the picture isn't crystal clear. It's not reckless. It's calculated risk-taking, combined with an open mind to course-correct later.

Instagram offers a powerful example. Founders Kevin Systrom and Mike Krieger originally launched it in 2010 as a location-based check-in app called Burbn. However, Systrom quickly realised the app was cluttered and unfocused. Instead of sticking with the original idea, he made a swift decision to strip the app down to its core: photo-sharing. Within weeks, the app was relaunched as Instagram, focusing exclusively on mobile photo sharing with filters that enhanced user images. This rapid pivot was undertaken without waiting for perfect market research or complete certainty. Instagram's team trusted their instincts, acted fast and iterated continuously based on genuine user insights.

This decisiveness helped Instagram capture the rapidly growing mobile social media market. Facebook took notice and acquired Instagram just two years after its launch for $1 billion, a staggering sum for such a young company. Kevin Systrom's ability to cut through uncertainty, focus on what mattered, and execute quickly allowed Instagram to become one of the world's most influential social networks.

To get decisive, set deadlines for your decisions, use frameworks like '70 per cent of info is enough', and remember: speed beats perfection, every single time.

Adaptability: When Stubbornness Isn't a Virtue

Stubbornness is the enemy of startups. Clinging to an idea like a lifebuoy when the market's screaming otherwise is a classic founder trap. If resilience is about bouncing back, adaptability is about changing your game plan when the playing field shifts. Founders who cling too tightly to original ideas risk missing new opportunities or worse, becoming obsolete.

Adaptable founders closely listen to customers, market trends and insights, and sometimes to their own gut. They aren't afraid to tweak, pivot or even overhaul their plans. They balance humility with confidence, staying rooted in their mission while remaining flexible in their approach.

Take FirstCry. Supam Maheshwari's journey is adaptability in action. A mechanical engineer from Delhi College of Engineering with an MBA from IIM Ahmedabad, he launched Brainvisa Technologies in 2000, raised ₹3 crore just before the dot-com crash, and survived by pivoting from a consumer test-prep model to a B2B before exiting in 2007. Those years ingrained cash discipline and resilience. In 2010, when he co-founded FirstCry with Amitava Saha, it wasn't a fixed idea but a response to a lived problem – the lack of reliable baby-care retail in India. As the business grew, FirstCry kept evolving: starting with a limited catalogue, moving early into omnichannel retail, building its own logistics, and expanding formats – all by listening to customers and reshaping the model as reality demanded.[4]

The smartest founders? They don't marry their first idea. They innovate in sync with their customers.

To sharpen adaptability, embrace feedback loops, run quick experiments, and keep your ego out of the decision room.[2]

Vision: The North Star That Guides You

Resilience, decisiveness and adaptability keep you in the game. But vision? Vision lets you rewrite the rules. A strong vision is more than just a catchy mission statement. It's a powerful mental map that guides your startup through chaos, helping you build something that lasts beyond trends and hype.

Vision is what separates a wanderer from a trailblazer. It's the big, bold picture that inspires your team and keeps your startup moving forward through fog and storms.

In 2010, India was still glued to cash. Digital wallets? They sounded like science fiction to the average user. But Vijay Shekhar Sharma, founder of Paytm, wasn't waiting for the country to be ready. He was preparing it anyway, envisioning a robust, mobile-first future.

At a time when India's digital infrastructure was patchy and smartphones were a luxury, Sharma imagined a world where a mobile phone could serve as your wallet, bank and storefront. People laughed. Some advised him to stick to safer, more 'Indian' ideas. But he bet on scale, trust and the invisible wave of digital transformation.[3]

His real moment came when demonetisation supercharged adoption in 2016. While others scrambled, Paytm soared. What appeared like luck was, in reality, preparation meeting foresight. Sharma didn't just build a product; he bet on a behaviour that hadn't happened yet, and when it did, Paytm wasn't playing catch-up. It was leading the parade.[4]

That's the vision. Not building for today. But building boldly, a little ahead of its time, and waiting for the world to catch up.

These four subtle powers within the core of a founder's character aren't stand-alone virtues; they reinforce each other in motion. Resilience builds the confidence to act; decisiveness sparks motion that demands adaptability; adaptability reshapes and refines the vision; and vision, in turn, strengthens resilience when storms hit.

The Mindset Shift

The founder's mindset isn't a fixed trait you're born with; it's a muscle you build every day through failures, wins and everything in between. Resilience turns pain into power. Decisiveness keeps you moving forward. Adaptability lets you surf the waves of change. Vision gives you a North Star to aim for.

Mix in emotional intelligence and self-awareness, and you've got a recipe for navigating the wild world of startups with confidence and clarity.

2

The Dare Mindset

Managing Risks and Fears

ENTREPRENEURSHIP ISN'T FOR THE faint of heart or the blindly brave. It's not about reckless leaps and yelling, 'Yahoo!' It's about making smart, deliberate, and sometimes gut-wrenching choices in the face of uncertainty.

Here's the truth: every iconic startup story has one thing in common. Risk. It's the native language of entrepreneurship. Think of Zerodha. They bet on discount broking when no one believed Indian traders would embrace online platforms. Take OYO Rooms which standardised budget hotels across India when travellers had low trust in small independent properties and hotel owners resisted brand control. Each of these moves looked improbable at first, but the risk opened new markets. Risk runs through them all.

But this is not the casino-table kind of risk. We're discussing informed, strategic and visionary risk. The kind where you don't just roll the dice. You know which battles to fight, what data to trust, and when to double down, even when everyone else plays it safe.

Mindset Cue: Founders don't wait for certainty; they create it.

The most successful founders aren't prophets. They act before the picture is clear. Certainty is a luxury startups can't afford. Wait for it, and you've already missed the bus, driven by someone hungrier than you.

Whether launching a new category, pivoting from a dead-end strategy, or entering an untested market, every major entrepreneurial move comes with uncertainty baked in. There's no app to calculate a 'safe-to-risk' ratio. There's only your vision, your gut and the data you can scrape together.

What separates founders who reach the sky from those who never leave the ground? How they deal with risk. The great ones don't avoid it. They assess it, embrace it, and harness it like a well-trained dragon.

That said, don't romanticise risk-taking. There's a razor-thin line between audacity and recklessness, between vision and delusion. Early-stage founders live in this zone of calculated chaos. You're not just building a product. You're betting your time, energy, sleep and sanity on a vision that doesn't exist yet. This chapter is your playbook for making those bets wisely.

The Psyche Behind Risk-Taking

Risk-taking isn't a 'go big or go home' macho mantra. It's a mix of science, psychology and self-awareness. It's knowing yourself, reading the situation, and moving forward despite fear. Uncertainty can feel paralysing because our brains crave safety. But progress comes only when we step past that comfort.

In general, our psyche is wired for *loss aversion*. We fear losing more than we enjoy winning. Losing $1,000 stings far more than gaining $1,000 feels good. This fear traps brilliant minds in safe jobs, scrolling YouTube about startups instead of building one. But entrepreneurs are wired differently. They still feel the fear of failure, but they weigh it against the cost of never trying, and, usually, the latter feels heavier. The founders who succeed don't ignore fear. They out-think it.

Take Reed Hastings, Netflix co-founder. In the early 2000s, Netflix rented DVDs and faced Blockbuster, the then market leader in the video-rental space, head-on. Streaming seemed like a distant prospect, suffocated by slow internet and low demand. But Hastings saw the future. He bet big on streaming and original content, even if it hurt their profitable DVD business. Many called it reckless. Today, that risk reshaped entertainment and made Netflix a household name. Not luck. Vision, conviction, and the courage to disrupt your own success.[1]

The Fine Line: Smart Versus Reckless

Let's not sugarcoat it. Not all risk is noble. Some risks are smart, meticulously analysed, strategically framed, and executed with precision. Others are dumb and reckless, born out of ego, desperation, or a desire to impress. The difference lies not in the size of the leap, but in the mindset behind it.

A calculated risk is like stepping off a cliff with operative knowledge of a parachute you tested yourself. It involves assessing altitude, planning, backup options, and a clear understanding of consequences. It's like saying, 'This could go wrong, but here's my mitigation plan.' On the other hand, reckless risk is leaping without looking, driven more by abrupt emotions than by insight. It often ends in regret, chaos, or collapse. Reckless risk is ego in a hoodie.

A textbook example of calculated risk is Jeff Bezos's decision to diversify Amazon's offerings beyond books. This wasn't a spur-of-the-moment move.

Bezos didn't build Amazon by waking up one day and shouting, 'Let's sell everything!' He meticulously studied consumer data, anticipated the evolution of e-commerce, and strategically expanded. From books to electronics, groceries and web services, every move was surgical. That's smart risk-taking. Bezos didn't gamble. He studied where online retail was heading, tested customer appetite, and prepared contingencies before expanding beyond books. His leap looked bold from the outside, but it was grounded in meticulous preparation. His calculated bets transformed Amazon into a global retail and tech giant.

Contrast this with Housing.com under Rahul Yadav.[2] Flush with investor money, Housing.com splurged on aggressive hiring, massive marketing spends, and over-the-top office spaces without a sustainable revenue model. Risk-taking turned into recklessness. Instead of building steady growth with customer value at the centre, ambition outran execution. Public spats, erratic leadership and impulsive decisions overshadowed the product. The result? Burned investor trust, stalled momentum, and eventually a forced exit. It wasn't boldness. It was chaos disguised as vision.

Dancing with Risk

Risk is part of the founder's DNA. The real question is how to embrace it without becoming a cautionary tale. Here's how modern founders can build a risk-ready mindset.

Start small. Test fast. Fail cheap. You don't need to quit your job or raise a million-dollar seed round to validate an idea. In fact, you shouldn't. Airbnb began with three air mattresses on a floor. Dropbox used nothing more than a simple explainer video before writing a single line of code. Think minimum viable products (MVPs), smoke tests and quick hacks. The goal is to get real feedback, not perfection. Learn without overcommitting.

Play the 'worst-case scenario' game. Ask yourself: *if this fails, what's the absolute worst that can happen? Can I live with it?* If the downside is survivable and the upside is meaningful, take the leap. That's exactly how Howard Schultz went all in on Starbucks. The risk was real, but so was the reward – global coffee domination.

Strip out emotion, replace it with evidence. Founders often fall in love with their ideas, but emotions cloud judgement. Data doesn't. Talk to users. Test assumptions. Study competitors. Even Tesla's move into China wasn't a wild bet. It was rooted in EV adoption trends, government backing and the potential for scale.[3]

Surround yourself with truth-tellers. Friends and family will cheer you on, but you need people who'll call out your blind spots. Mentors, advisors and early customers will tell you when your pricing model is broken or your landing page looks like a school project. Their feedback grounds your vision in reality.

Finally, train for emotional resilience. Risk isn't only about projections and numbers. It shows up in the downtime after a rejected pitch, in the delays you can't control, and in the doubt that creeps in during late nights. It tests both your plans and your patience. The difference between founders who burn out and those who bounce back lies in emotional habits. Meditate. Sleep well. Eat better. Talk to other founders. These rituals aren't fluff. They're survival strategies. Risk won't disappear, but with the right mindset, it stops being a threat and becomes your engine for growth.

Mindset Cue: Vision without feedback is hallucination.

Let's talk about a homegrown power move. In 2010, Dr Swati Piramal and Ajay Piramal undertook an unprecedented step. They sold their wildly successful pharmaceutical business. The market gasped. 'They sold the golden goose!' critics cried. But here's what they saw: the opportunity to reshape their portfolio into something broader and future-forward. Healthcare analytics, real estate and financial services. Less intriguing? Maybe. More strategic? Absolutely.[4]

Today, the Piramal Group is thriving. Why? Because that 'risky' move was actually a calculated pivot based on macroeconomic insights, internal strengths and long-term vision. It's a masterclass in risk as transformation, not just disruption.

The Mindset Shift

Risk-taking isn't about losing objectivity in pursuit of your egoistic fulfilment. It's an ongoing internal negotiation between logic and fear, vision and doubt, ambition and humility. Risk is a tool.

Used poorly, risk wrecks startups. Exercised wisely, it makes legends. The founders who champion their game don't shy away from the unknown. They step into it with discipline, clarity and preparation.

So, before your next big decision, ask: is this leap based on data or desperation? Is it grounded in strategy or fantasy? Am I doing this to grow or to prove something? Because in startups, the game doesn't reward the most fearless. It rewards the most prepared, self-aware and adaptable. So, welcome to the dance with uncertainty. Learn the steps, keep your feet under you and don't forget to enjoy the rhythm.

3

The Right-Fit Mindset

The Founder Marrying the Market

As they say, 'Before you chase product–market fit, make sure you fit the market.'

Early-stage founders often leap into building solutions without checking if they belong in the arena they're entering. The Right-Fit Mindset is simple yet revolutionary: you must align your passion, skills and lived experience with your target customers' real needs. When that alignment clicks, everything else, from product design to go-to-market, falls into place with far less friction.

When your own pain points mirror those of your customers or buyers, you instinctively know which edges to sharpen and which experiments to kill. That lived empathy becomes your secret product spec. You don't add a '*nice-to-have*' because it sounds trendy, you solve a '*need-to-have*' because you've felt the burn yourself. That doesn't necessarily mean you must have a personal pain point to build a venture; rather, it simply means you must relate very personally and mentally to the problem you are solving.

Mindset Cue: You must have your foot into the problem you're willing to solve for your customers. That's where alignment hits.

Conversely, misaligned founders become reactive builders, chasing every odd request like a game of feature ping-pong. 'What if it had this too?' They say *yes* to everything because they don't have a filter grounded in personal insight. Lacking that inner compass, their product drifts, shaped more by noise than need. And that's a mindset mismatch you can't afford to ignore.

The Right-Fit Mindset flips this script. You don't just build for users; you are the user. Every tweak feels urgent. Every bug fix feels personal. That 'lived connection' creates faster feedback loops and clearer decisions. When you finally ship, you won't need to convince people why it matters. They'll feel your conviction in every feature you deliver because it was built by someone who gets it.

So essentially, why does founder–market fit matter? For three core reasons.

First, it's fuel for the long haul. Startups aren't 100-metre sprints. They're ultra-marathons with potholes, detours and zero roadside cheering. If you're not deeply into the market you're serving, you'll burn out the moment it stops being exciting (trust me, it will happen). Founders who obsess over their market's weird workflows, broken tools and inner politics have a natural edge. They stay curious, even when traction is slow or funding dries up. Chasing hot sectors just because VCs love them? That's like marrying for money; it is unsustainable when times get rough.

Second, it introduces firsthand empathy. When you've lived or have *internalised* the problem, you don't need to run surveys to understand user pain. You've been that frustrated customer, wrestling with clunky software or navigating inefficient supply chains. That insight helps you define the problem with surgical precision and craft solutions that actually stick. It's why former teachers build better edtech, and ex-finance folks reinvent fintech. The intuition that comes from experience is something no consultant report can replace.

Lastly, you establish credibility on Day 1. The moment you open your mouth people size you up: 'Does this founder get us?' And when you speak their lingo, share their pain, and recognise the problem before they do, you earn trust fast. Early hires rally behind your mission. Customers are more willing to bet on your beta. Even reluctant partners lean in. You're not just pitching a solution. You're embodying the market's story. And that authenticity is magnetic.

For founders who have already embarked on their startup journey, it's imperative to assess whether they are playing on the right ground or not. Sometimes, the clearest path forward starts with knowing what not to ignore. Here's how to spot the red flags when you're not in sync with your market.

#Red Flag 1: You Google About the Market More Than Experiencing It.

If you're constantly researching what your target users care about rather than instinctively knowing it, you may be an outsider. There exist fair chances that you've skimmed blogs and memorised stats, but you've never walked in your customer's shoes or better yet, sat in their chair. Sure, research is important. But if it's your primary compass, not a supplement to real experience, you're building from the outside in. Founder–market fit feels more like muscle memory, not Wikipedia rabbit holes.

#Red Flag 2: Customer Calls Feel Like Interviews, Not Conversations.

You're driven by the 'cool factor' of an industry rather than the urge to resolve a burning pain. Every time you speak to a user, you should feel like you're finishing each other's sentences. If it feels stiff, like you're probing a stranger instead of jamming with a peer, maybe you're not close enough to the core problem. Empathy isn't just understanding pain points; it's assessing and internalising them before they're spoken.

#Red Flag 3: The Product Excites You More Than the Impact.

You might be pumped about the solution you've built and the innovation packed in it. But are you actually invested in why it should matter to those for whom it is built? Founders who have market fit don't talk features; they talk impact. If you're more excited by the tech stack than the user transformation, your heart may be in the wrong room.

#Red Flag 4: Your Road Map Is a Request List.

If you're building based on every customer whim without a gut sense of what to say no to, you might be misaligned.

Founders with strong market fit have an internal compass. They listen, sure. But they're not swayed. They lead the market instead of merely reacting to it.

For instance, Color Labs, the photo-sharing startup that raised $41 million before launch.[1] Despite a star-studded team, they never truly understood the emotional dynamics underlying mobile photo-sharing. The founders weren't deeply embedded in the Instagram generation. They were outsiders trying to manufacture virality. The result? A flashy product that no one felt a need for. The tech worked, but the resonance didn't. Users didn't just fail to care; they failed to get it. That's the cost of skipping founder–market alignment.

If you find yourself chasing every shiny feature idea, unsure of what really matters to your user or worse, struggling to remember the 'why' behind your market proposition, you may not be building from the inside out. And that's a mindset mismatch you can't afford to ignore.

Startups are hard enough. Don't make it harder by picking a problem that doesn't belong to you. The right-fit arena is where your personal edge meets a market's urgent need. It's not just about passion, it's about proximity. Have you breathed the problem? Do you speak the unspoken language of your target user? If not, you're an outsider trying to fix what you don't fully understand.

Look at Notion and Evernote. Both set out to become the all-in-one digital workspace.[2] But Notion's founders, Ivan Zhao and Simon Last, were designer–developers building for other designer–developers. They deeply felt the pain of context-switching between scattered tools and cumbersome workflows. That first-hand insight became their advantage. Their product felt like it was built by someone like you.

Evernote, on the other hand, while early to the space, eventually lost product focus and became bloated with features aimed at everyone and no one. Their team drifted away from a core user identity, and in the absence of a strong founder–market resonance, innovation slowed, and user love faded.[3]

The difference? Notion was built from inside the arena. They didn't just identify a market gap. They occupied it. And that closeness allowed them to iterate with nuance, win user evangelism, and scale with soul.

Mindset Cue: When your story overlaps with your customer's struggle, you move faster, sound more credible, and build what truly sticks.

The Three Tests of Founder–Market Fit

Before you bet your life on a startup, check if the market would bet on you, too.

Having a founder–market fit isn't a vibe; it's a validation. It shows up not in your pitch deck, but in how naturally you understand the problem, talk to customers, and make product calls. Here are three simple but telling tests to know if you belong in the arena you're stepping into:

1. The Language Test: Can you talk like your users without sounding like a tourist? Real founder–market fit isn't about jargon, it's about knowing the context behind the words. A founder building for healthcare who can decode EHR pain points or reimbursement workflows? That's fluency. If you're Googling acronyms mid-call, it's a red flag.
2. The Rolodex Test: Can you line up ten people in your close network who'll take your call today and experience your product from proximity to give you your first fair reality check? This litmus test shows if you're entering the market from the inside. Again, it shouldn't be an echo chamber testing where friends or advocates give you warm nods but no honest feedback. Seek out harsh critics.
3. The 'Would You Use It?' Test: If your own product doesn't excite you, why should it excite anyone else?

> Founders with real fit build for themselves or their past selves. Think of Melanie Perkins, Canva's founder, who taught design and saw firsthand how inaccessible design tools were for non-designers. That frustration became fuel, and Canva became a rocket ship.[4]

Now contrast that with founders who chase a 'hot, trendy' sector purely because VCs are writing cheques, say an AI-powered fintech startup launched by someone who's never stepped inside a bank or handled lending risk. Their MVPs often feel hollow, their positioning generic, and users sniff it out fast.

True founder–market fit isn't just about credibility; it gives you compounding insight. You learn faster, pivot smarter, and speak to your customer like an ally, not a vendor.

The Mindset Shift

The real turning point isn't when your MVP clicks, it's when your *identity* does. Great startups aren't just built on solving problems; they're built by founders who feel the weight of those problems in their bones. You're not just building software, a service, or a pitch deck. You're building for people like you with the same headaches, hopes and habits. That's where the Right-Fit Mindset kicks in. It's when your personal obsession overlaps with public need.

And suddenly, you're not guessing the market. *You are the market. That's the shift from chasing trends to becoming the trendsetter.* From asking, 'Will they care?' to hearing them say, 'Finally, someone who gets it.'

Your unfair advantage isn't your deck or your demo. It's that your story already belongs to the customer you're serving. And when that happens, building doesn't feel forced. It feels inevitable.

4

The Action Mindset

Challenging Mental Barriers

EVERY FOUNDER STARTS WITH an idea, a spark, a sketch, a pitch in the shower. Whether it's about disrupting an old industry, solving a problem that bugs you now and then, or just building something cool that the world hasn't seen before – ideas come easy. Action, execution? That's where the real game begins.

Some founders dive in head first, tweaking and adapting as they go. Others get stuck in the waiting room of overthinking, unsure whether to move forward, pivot, or give up altogether. The biggest challenge for a startup isn't execution, it's hesitation.

The gap between *what's in your head* and *what's out in the world* is usually filled with some sneaky mental barriers like fear of failure, perfectionism, procrastination, imposter syndrome, and so on. These aren't just buzzwords, they're the invisible handbrakes that hold back even the brightest minds from making meaningful progress.

This chapter focuses on recognising the three most critical mental blocks, understanding where they come from, and most importantly, learning how to beat them with action.

Mental Barrier #1: The Fear of Failure

Let's call it what it is – the most crippling dream-killer for entrepreneurs. And it doesn't discriminate whether you're building a next-gen AI app or starting a cold brew cart, fear of failure shows up, loud and uninvited.

We live in a startup culture that celebrates glitzy wins, funding rounds, unicorn status, and glowing headlines. What rarely makes the cut? The 27 failures that came before. As a result, many founders hesitate to act, worrying about rejection, judgement, or simply their ideas falling flat.

How Fear Freezes Founders

- **Over-analysis Mode:** You catch yourself endlessly refining a slide deck or rewriting code, waiting for that magical 'perfect' version. Meanwhile, the world moves on. You convince yourself that more research will help, but really, it's fear masquerading as your fixation for thoroughness. It leads to inaction, and founders get caught up in doubting and overthinking every decision.

- **Infinite Validation:** Validation is critical. But if you spend six months 'validating' and never actually launch, you become your own worst enemy. You'll read one more article, talk to one more friend, or tweak one more pixel ... until the last validator affirms. You delay the launch, caught in a cycle of infinite refinement, postponing market launch, waiting for 'the right moment' and final validation just to be sure, only to end up never being sure.
- **Inner Critic Overload:** When you imagine potential failure like losing money, embarrassing yourself in front of your peers, or receiving negative feedback, it chips away at your confidence. Self-doubt feasts on doubts. 'What if this fails? Maybe I'm not made for this!' and suddenly you question whether you even deserve to try or if you're 'founder material' at all.

The foundational shift is to see failure not as an endpoint, but as data. Call it 'feedback' instead of 'failure'. Moreover, adopting the 'Fail Fast, Learn Faster' mindset can empower founders to build their confidence. When you frame it that way, every misstep becomes a lesson, not a roadblock.

Look at Airbnb.[1] In their early days, they were broke, rejected by investors, and had no traction. So what did they do? They sold Obama O's and Cap'n McCain's cereal during the 2008 election to fund their startup. Sounds ridiculous? But it worked. More importantly, it helped them stay viable long enough to iterate, learn, and build one of the most disruptive companies of the decade.

Tactical Steps to Win over This Psychological Barrier

1. Flip the Fear: As humans, we are wired to catastrophise. Our minds default to, 'What if I fail? What if everyone laughs? What if I lose money?' But here's a curveball: what if it works? What if your product gains traction, your idea goes viral, or a user sends that 'This changed my life' email? Train your brain to obsess over the upside of a scenario, not just the downside. Fear imagines disaster; founders imagine opportunity. That simple mental flip can turn hesitation into momentum.
2. Set Micro-Experiments: Instead of 'I have to build a complete product', commit to a simple test: a one-page landing page, a short survey, or a quick demo video. These micro-experiments give you real, on-demand feedback without risking your entire budget or reputation.
3. Celebrate Small Failures: Make this a team ritual. If a marketing email tanks or a new feature crashes, acknowledge it publicly then share what you learned. When your squad sees that mistakes are okay (even expected), it builds a culture where fear can't thrive.
4. Lean on Peer Accountability: Find a founder buddy or join a mastermind group. Commit to sharing your next risky move. Say, 'I'm launching my MVP on Friday.' When the others know your plan, you'll feel extra motivation to push through fear. Accountability helps you take action.

Mindset Cue: Don't shy away from failure. Study it, embrace it, and build from it. Shift from panic to possibility. And you'll sail!

Mental Barrier #2: Perfectionism

If fear of failure is the loud wrecker, perfectionism is its quieter, suit-wearing cousin. It pretends to be your friend, whispering classic one-liners like 'Let's polish this more', 'We're almost there', or the infamous 'It's not ready yet'.

This trap *feels* like productivity but often isn't. Many founders convince themselves that unless the product is flawless, it's not ready.

Perfectionism convinces smart founders to believe that their product requires only one more tweak before launch. One more feature. One more redesign. One more pivot to chase 'the perfect version'. But in reality? It's never perfect.

As a founder, you definitely want your product to shine. You want the world to see its best version, not a rough draft. The problem is that the world won't wait until you are done with your best. And that can result in endless delays, lost opportunities, and, at worst, can cost you your venture itself.

Perfectionism stalls execution in subtle yet dangerous ways. It can make you delay your launch, stoking fear and judgement about an 'unfinished' product. It can push you to overbuild or add features no one asked for, believing that 'more is better', while drifting away from what truly matters, the core problem your product is meant to solve. At times, it can lead you to hide or shy away from feedback, polishing endlessly rather than testing boldly in the real market.

Let's be honest: most unicorn startups didn't start with flawless products. They launched fast, learned faster, and let real users shape the evolution.

Mindset Cue: Perfectionism is fear dressed elegantly. If you never launch, no one can criticise you, but no one can love what you've built either.

MVP Over OCD

A minimum viable product (MVP) is the antidote to your inner 'OCD' – that obsessive compulsion for details – reminding you that progress beats polishing every pixel to perfection. It's not about being sloppy, it's about being smart. The Pareto Principle suggests that 80 per cent of results often come from 20 per cent of effort. So instead of obsessing over pixel-perfect logos or ten extra features, focus on delivering *just enough* value to test your core hypothesis. *That's the MVP mindset.*

As a founder, you have to have confidence that you're not shipping junk. You're shipping just enough value to test your riskiest assumptions. The MVP is your early invite to the feedback party, and trust me, the guest list matters more than the lighting.

Mindset Cue: Often, simple, frugal launches win while pretty procrastination loses.

Reid Hoffman, founder of LinkedIn, popularly comments, 'If you're not embarrassed by the first version of your product, you've launched too late.'

Founders need to embrace the idea that making progress is far more important than striving for perfection. Releasing an MVP into market is a smarter move. By gathering real user data, you can make informed improvements instead of getting stuck in endless refinement behind closed doors. It's all about execution, not perfection, that propels successful startups ahead.

Tactical Steps to Win over This Psychological Barrier

1. Apply the 80/20 Rule Like a Founder, not a Neurotic Artist: Ask yourself, what's the 20 per cent of this product that will deliver 80 per cent of the value? Focus on that. Build that. Launch that. Don't obsess over the login animation when your core problem is getting users to sign up.
2. Replace 'Perfect' with 'Proven': Don't chase perfect features. Aim for features that prove something valuable, such as 'Will users pay for this?' or 'Will they come back tomorrow?' Let data, not your inner critic, dictate what gets improved.

3. Time-Box the Tinkering: Set deadlines. Not just for the launch, but also for decision-making. Give yourself one day to decide on a feature, two days to build, and zero days for second-guessing. Perfectionists love open timelines. Omit them.
4. Build What They Care About: Remember, users don't care about your font style. Most early adopters don't care if your button is round or flat. They care if your product solves their problem. Focus on utility, not vanity. Your audience wants solutions, not elegance – at least not early on.
5. Track Progress, Not Polish: Keep a log of what you've shipped, tested, learned and improved. Celebrate small launches. Every line of code, every small upgrade in production, is a punch in the face of perfectionism.

Mental Barrier #3: Procrastination

This one's sneaky and deceptive. Procrastination wears many disguises – I'm still validating, waiting on the designer, need more funds, resources aren't perfect, just need to research more. Sounds smart. But often, it's just worthless delays dressed as productivity.

Unlike perfectionism, which is often more conscious and goal-oriented, procrastination subtly erodes momentum, leaving founders stuck in the planning or postponing stage while others move ahead.

Psychologists say procrastination isn't laziness. It's often a stress response, especially to uncertainty or fear of failure. That means your brain isn't saying, 'I don't care.' It's saying, 'I care too much, and I'm overwhelmed.' Here, we'd better face a straight question: *why do founders procrastinate*?

Execution Anxiety: The Real Enemy of Momentum

Well, procrastination isn't about being lazy or careless. For founders, it's usually tied to deeper emotional conflicts and cognitive distortions, such as:

- Fear and Ambiguity: Launching a startup means navigating ambiguity. Many founders delay action because they aren't sure what comes next, and the brain avoids discomfort by prioritising easier or more familiar tasks.
- Emotional Perfectionism: Some founders fear that if they're not 'in the right mindset' or feeling motivated, they'll mess it up. So they wait for that ideal burst of inspiration and energy, which may never arrive.
- Overwhelming Scope: Startups involve juggling multiple priorities – team-building, product development, marketing and finances. The sheer magnitude of responsibility can lead to a shutdown, where founders postpone action to avoid being overwhelmed.
- Avoiding the Tough: Founders forgo uncomfortable tasks like sales or fundraising. And the dependent priority tasks get strangled. It's not laziness; it's an easy-go-lucky attitude problem.

Take Shopify.[2] Founder Tobias Lütke could have spent years refining the perfect platform before launching. Instead, he built the core functionalities and went live quickly, learning from real user behaviour. In contrast, countless e-commerce tools with potentially better codebases never saw the light of day because their founders delayed too long. Remember, decisive action beats delayed perfection.

Tactical Steps to Win over This Psychological Barrier

1. Break the Inertia with 'Micro-actions': Procrastination thrives on the illusion that a task is too big. Break major tasks into micro-actions that can be done in under ten minutes. Don't aim to 'launch a company'. Instead, aim to 'write a one-line pitch' or 'set up a landing page'.
2. Create Structured Routines: The most prolific founders don't rely on motivation. They build systems and

routines that enforce consistency. Having a 'Launch Hour' every day, when you only work on outward execution, can beat the tendency to tinker endlessly behind the scenes.

3. Employ the Pomodoro Technique: It's a time management method where you work in focused 25-minute intervals (called 'Pomodoros') followed by a five-minute break. After four Pomodoros, take a longer 15- to 30-minute break. It boosts productivity by reducing burnout and distractions. Once you begin, momentum usually follows.
4. Build a 'Launch-First' Culture: Whether you're solo or have a team, establish a culture where launching, shipping and iterating quickly are the norm. Celebrate experiments, not just successes.
5. Install External Accountability Loops: Share your goals publicly on LinkedIn, with a mentor, or through founder communities. When you make a public commitment, you introduce external accountability, which helps mitigate procrastination.
6. Treat Anxiety as a Performance Signal: Reframe your fear-driven delays as signals that you're stepping outside your comfort zone, and that's exactly where growth happens. Just as athletes experience pre-race nerves, founders often experience mental resistance just before a breakthrough.

The Mindset Shift

Ideas are everywhere and with everyone. Execution? That's gold. A brilliant idea is just the beginning; it only matters when it connects with the world. The founders who win aren't always the smartest; they're the ones who *act*. They know they'll mess up. They accept that early versions will be rough and raw. But they also know you can't learn from a product that's still stuck in a notebook or buried in a Google Doc.

So founders, move fast. Break these mental chains. Launch the draft version. Talk to users. Learn from the hits and the misses. Progress beats perfection. Always.

5

The Execution Mindset

Dodging the Five Traps

Every founder starts out with a spark, a big idea, a bold dream, and caffeine coursing through their veins. But passion, as inspiring as it is, won't save your startup from extinction. The startup graveyard is full of brilliant ideas and sprint plans that died not from a lack of innovation, but blundered execution.

In startup land, failing isn't fatal. But repeating rookie mistakes? That's the slippery slope that is impossible get back up from. This chapter is your warning siren. Your execution GPS. A friendly warning on potential traps you might face while you begin to build and execute. After all, beyond the media's obsession with valuation headlines, most will agree that the startup game is more like Temple Run than Candy Crush. It's not about colourful wins. It's about dodging obstacles and staying in the race.

Straightaway, let's dissect the five most critical execution traps that can potentially choke your startup. And more importantly, how to avoid them like a founder with vision and sound judgement.

Trap #1: Neglecting Market Validation

Enamoured with their creation, too often, founders are like, 'If we build it, they will come!' In reality, no, they won't. They'll scroll past you on Instagram. Falling in love with your idea is easy and, to some degree, good. But who cares what you love! The market cares whether you solve a real problem or offer something irresistible. That's what builds businesses. Too many founders skip the hard stuff like talking to real people, and jump straight into comfortable assumptions.

Quibi, founded by Hollywood mogul Jeffrey Katzenberg and tech veteran Meg Whitman, was a short-form video streaming platform that raised a staggering $1.75 billion before fizzling out faster than a TikTok trend and shutting down in just six months.[1] It set out to redefine mobile entertainment with its premium offerings. Despite having Hollywood stars and a war chest of investor capital, they forgot to ask the critical question: *do people even want this?* Spoiler: they didn't. With free, addictive content already available on YouTube, Instagram and TikTok, Quibi's paid model was the digital equivalent of selling bottled water next to a river. The setback stemmed not only from execution missteps but also from a fundamental misreading of consumer behaviour. The company jumped into production and marketing without first validating its assumptions. And that ended in a swift free fall!

Now, how do you dodge out of this trap? Validate your idea before spending a rupee. Build a scrappy MVP just enough to test the core promise. Don't rush to raise funds without proof or traction. Talk to real users, not your co-founder or college gang. Remember Dropbox's explainer video? That's validation done right. Proof before product, traction before tech.[2]

Trap #2: Building the Wrong Team

Mindset Cue: An early 'no' from the market is cheaper than a late-stage implosion.

Bad hires mean broken foundations. The truth is your startup isn't going to build itself. And sadly you can't build it alone. The earlier you realise this, the better. But that doesn't call for hasty hiring in the rush to build fast, grow quicker, and look legit. That's the mistake many founders make early on that haunts them later: hiring in haste and regretting it at scale.

In early-stage chaos, it's tempting to grab whoever's available, fill seats, or worse – hire your college buddy who once 'had a cool app idea'. But hiring based on convenience, speed or familiarity rather than capability and cultural alignment is like building a skyscraper on quicksand. Things look fine until they don't.

Startups live or die on their teams. And when you put the wrong people in the wrong seats, you're not just risking operational mess-ups. You're inviting toxic dynamics, fuzzy decision-making and internal misfires that will take ten times as much energy to clean up as it took to create. Misaligned hires don't just slow down your rocket ship; they crash it.

Let's take the infamous Theranos implosion. Elizabeth Holmes promised to revolutionise healthcare with Theranos. But instead of assembling a team that could challenge assumptions and ground the vision in real science, she surrounded herself with loyalists, the yes-men who echoed her hype, not truth. The result? A biotech unicorn valued at over $9 billion became a cautionary tale, embroiled in criminal fraud charges.

Theranos didn't just lack scientific validation; it lacked people who could speak up. That's the cost of building an echo chamber instead of a team.[3]

A great startup team isn't just a bunch of smart resumes. It's a tight squad of believers, builders and boundary-pushers. People who share the mission sharpen each other's thinking and challenge bad ideas before the market does. As a founder, your job is to curate this chemistry. Such a team has a visibly enormous impact on its founder's decision-making, overall mindset, and the business at large.

Now, how do you guard against this trap? Simple. Hire slow, but fire decisively. Hire for mission fit, not just fancy résumés. Test people on real tasks rather than relying on feel-good interviews. Build a culture that questions assumptions and doesn't mindlessly conform. When someone's a poor fit, act fast, be kind, but be firm. Define each role clearly; ambiguous roles always lead to ambiguous results. Certainly, beware of emotionally biased hires. They often break more than they build.

Your dream team isn't a squad of clones. It's a cocktail of builders, critics, doers and dreamers with just enough friction to spark brilliance, not burnout. We'll discuss team building in detail in later chapters.

Trap #3: Scaling Too Soon

'Let's go global!' Hold up. Have you even gone *local*?

Growth feels good. Really good. So good, in fact, that many founders treat it like a badge of honour – more funds, more hires, more ads, more cities, more chaos! But here's the kicker. Growth that happens too early is like putting nitro in a go-kart. It might move fast, but it's going to crash hard.

Too many startups shift into fifth gear before the engine's even broken in. They chase headlines rather than health, investors instead of insights. The product's still in beta, the team's half-baked, the customers are confused, but hey, we've got office spaces in four time zones!

Scaling before you've nailed the product–market fit is like pouring gasoline on a fire you can't control, or worse, on a campfire that isn't even lit.

For instance, Fab.com went from startup darling to cautionary tale in record time.[4] At its peak, the e-commerce venture reached a remarkable valuation of $1 billion, fuelled by swift international growth across various markets. But that valuation was built on shaky ground.[5] Massive hiring, aggressive international expansion, marketing spend without a working revenue model, weak customer retention and a marketing budget that could fund a small country – they chased scale without substance, and the flame went out faster than a flash sale. Fab went from 'next big thing' to 'what happened?' in no time.

Mindset Cue: Scaling isn't about how fast you grow. It's about how well you grow.

A startup isn't a balloon. You can't just keep inflating it and expect it not to pop at some point. Build operational maturity before geographic insanity.

Now, how to dodge this trap? Well, start small and grow sharply. Nail your niche before even thinking of tinkering with global domination. If it works in one city, test it in another. Track real traction, such as revenue, retention and genuine demand. If you don't have these, keep the jetpack grounded.

Scale systems, not chaos. Build processes that can scale before adding more people. Lock in your unit economics. Know exactly what each customer costs and what each brings. Reject vanity metrics as followers don't pay the bills; customers do. Don't fake progress with paid virality.

Build cash-flow confidence. If your business can't breathe without fresh investor oxygen every quarter, you're not ready to scale. Look for proof, not hype. If your product's flying off the shelves, then it's time to build a bigger shelf. If not, pause, refine and repeat.

Think Airbnb and Uber. Both started small, tested in micro-markets, refined through real feedback, and only then scaled to the moon.

Mindset Cue: Startup growth isn't a race. It's a staircase. Take one solid step at a time.

Trap #4: Ignoring Customer Voices

'Ah! We know what users want.' Yes, only if assumptions and affirmations could sail a startup.

At times, founders get so obsessed with their idea and product that they launch with the blind prophecy that 'the whole world is waiting for it'. Once launched, they forget to ask the most important question: *does anyone else actually care?*

When customer feedback doesn't match the founder's fantasy, it's too often brushed aside. Some founders treat feedback like spam. They block it, delete it, or worse, brush it away with ego-laced logic. But the brutal truth? The market always wins. If your users are trying to tell you something, the worst thing you can do for your startup is to ignore what they have to say.

The result? You end up building a shiny product solving a problem no one really has. That's not innovation, that's self-deception. You romanticise your vision and start building in an echo chamber. Real feedback often feels like criticism and is invariably muted. You launched something customers didn't ask for, didn't need, or frankly, didn't understand. And by the time reality hits, your pockets are already burned. This founder's ignorance squanders already measured resources, creates a mismatch with the market, and ultimately leads to the business's downfall.

Understanding customer insights is essential for figuring out if an idea truly resonates with the market or if it requires tweaks to align more closely with the needs of its target audience.

Let's take Google Glass.[6] A futuristic, AR-powered piece of eyewear. Brilliant tech, blinded by its own hype. On paper, Google Glass looked like it had teleported straight from the future. In reality, it showed up uninvited, overpriced, and for some, quite creepy. It promised innovation but delivered awkward stares, privacy panic, and a whole lot of 'Wait... are you recording me right now?'

Early users didn't hold back. Voices erupted: 'It's uncomfortable'; 'It's invasive'; 'It's trying too hard.' Privacy concerns shot up like red flags in a minefield. People don't love being secretly recorded during their lunch break. The design appeared clunky. The daily use-case? Questionable. Still, Google marched forward, seemingly thinking, 'It's revolutionary, and people will *get it* eventually.' They didn't.

Owing to terrible timing and even worse feedback management, the market soon gave the verdict rejecting Google Glass as awkward, expensive and socially weird. Even then, Google refused to budge and pressed launch anyway. Result? The product tanked. Instead of traction, they got friction. Glass flopped as an expensive science project that now lives in the Museum of Over-Engineered Things.

On the flip side, Slack was born from a failed game. Twitter is a pivot from a dying podcast platform to micro-posting.

Mindset Cue: Even the most unimaginable tech won't stick if it doesn't solve a real problem. Innovation means nothing if it forgets to invite the user to the party.

Both products made it big because their teams paid attention to what actually worked for their users, even if it wasn't part of the original plan. The common thread? They *watched* their users, *listened* to feedback, and *moved* when the signs were clear.

Now, how do you guard against this trap? You treat feedback as fuel, not friction. As a founder, you must build in tight beta loops and talk to early adopters often. Pivot based on real signals, not propelled by ego or working on an assumption. You must read, analyse and build around actual user behaviour. Accept that your big idea might only be the opening bid, not the final offer. Assumption is the most expensive fibre of your product. Great founders don't just solve assumed problems; they listen, adapt and evolve.

Mindset Cue: Your customers are your co-founders. They just don't have equity. Take their voices very seriously.

Trap #5: Mismanaging Money

It's shocking how fast a startup can go from 'we just raised $10 million' to 'we can't pay our people'.

One of the most common ways startups crash and die is by running out of cash and realising it only when it's too late. Many founders overspend on the shiny stuff like swanky offices, pointless perks, overpriced ads, etc. Others undermine the boring but vital stuff such as unit economics, margins and cash flow. They overlook a simple truth that revenue, not funding rounds, sustains a startup. The result? A beautiful bonfire built entirely of investor money. A projection-less, directionless ride that ends in a predictable crash.

Too often, there's this dangerous mindset: *'We'll raise the next round before we run out.'*

Let's rewind to the dot-com era, when Pets.com raised a whopping $300 million. With cash to burn, they went all in with Super Bowl ads, massive discounts, free shipping on giant dog food bags, and a mascot puppet. But no business model made sense. Revenue couldn't keep up with the burn, margins were laughable, and customers weren't sticking around. Within two years, the company filed for bankruptcy.

Mindset Cue: Money isn't fuel unless it's used wisely. It can spoil you as a founder to engage in fireworks for fun until there's nothing left to light.

Here is how you can dodge this fatal mindset trap.

Know your burn rate (the speed at which a startup spends its cash reserves before becoming profitable) like your blood pressure. If you don't track how fast you're spending versus earning, you're not running a business, you're gambling. Obsess over your runway. If you don't know how many months you can survive without new funding, panic triggers and plans disappear. Thus, forecast with vigilance.

Early on, spend like a bootstrapped monk, even if you're a funded mogul. Go lean. Every rupee, every dollar, must deliver tangible returns, either by attracting customers or retaining them. And when needed, raise capital but out of purpose, not panic or for showbiz. Think like Amazon, not Pets.com. One played the long game. The other burned bright and burned out.

Financial discipline isn't optional; it's your startup's life jacket. Don't build castles in the cloud with no cash on the ground. Real founders learn to stretch a rupee like it's elastic. Keep the burn in check, track your numbers religiously, and remember: it's better to be boringly profitable than excitingly bankrupt.

The Mindset Shift

Mistakes? You'll make them. Traps? All will inevitably appear. That's baked into the startup game. But repeating avoidable, obvious, already-warned-you-before mistakes? Or getting trapped in mindset errors? That's not hustle, that's a headless sprint.

The best founders stay alert. They study business failures as much as they study success stories. They test. They listen. They adapt. And most importantly, they execute with intention, not just adrenaline. If you can dodge these execution traps, you won't just survive, you'll outlive, outgrow and out-execute 90 per cent of the pack.

6

The Focus Mindset

Cutting Through Noise

At the heart of every legendary startup isn't just a flashy product, a quirky mascot, or a vigilant action – it's a vision that actually means something. A real one. Not a buzzword recipe cooked up for your investor deck, but a clear, gutsy and compelling direction that screams, 'This is where we're headed, and here's why it matters.'

More than corporate fluff, your vision is your North Star. It unites the team around a mission that matters. It guides every decision, keeping distractions out of the lane. It weatherproofs the company against market chaos. And it keeps you anxiously proactive, razor-focused on the path ahead without being distracted by transient attractions.

Without a grounded vision, you're running blind, dodging the real 'whys', and building without a sense of purpose.

Vision isn't about throwing darts at future trends. It's your startup's internal GPS, helping you make smarter decisions. In a world where the market can pivot overnight, *your vision is both your anchor in the storm and your compass in the fog*. It keeps you from drifting when things get tough, and, undoubtedly, things do get tough as the ship sails deeper. It's the answer to all the 'whys' behind your decisions, your directions.

When you don't have one, you find yourself just reacting, ping-ponging from trend to trend, pivoting with every LinkedIn hot take, and building features just because your competitor did. That's not called strategy. That's panic wearing a product–market fit coat.

That's where vision needs to marry a relentless partner. *Focus*. Focus keeps the action abreast and in sync with the original yet evolving vision. That's where the magic begins. It protects vision from derailment, from losing sight of your original reasoning – the core objectivity behind what you are building and why.

Vision does not exist only in the psyche. With focus, it builds the courage to pick a meaningful direction and stay the course, even when it's not the centre of attention. It's what turns startups from 'we're building an app' to 'we're building a movement'. And when that vision is dialled in? Every decision on features, hires, partnerships and pivots gets finer and better. Let's see how vision and focus dynamics act in startups.

Vision: The North Star

When OpenAI began its journey, generative AI was largely confined to research labs and academic papers. The idea that everyday users would converse with AI, generate code, create content, or solve complex problems in seconds felt distant and experimental.

Sam Altman and the team didn't wait for full regulatory clarity or perfect infrastructure; they envisioned a future where AI would become a daily productivity companion for millions. What began as research into large language models evolved into widely accessible AI tools used by students, developers, creators and enterprises globally. Their vision? Build safe and broadly beneficial artificial intelligence. Their bet? Human-AI collaboration would become foundational to modern work.

They continued backing that vision even when scaling costs were massive and scepticism around AI misuse was high. The clarity of that North Star turned breakthrough research into a mainstream shift in how the world works.

> **Mindset Cue: Vision doesn't wait for perfect conditions. It creates them by daring to sketch a future others missed seeing.**

Let's take Elon Musk, someone who is known for pushing the boundaries of possibility. He didn't just make electric cars; he reimagined the whole energy ecosystem. From solar roofs to gigafactories and battery storage, Tesla's vision has been unapologetically expansive; it remains so.[1] It's not just 'cars'; it's clean energy, software, updates and autonomy built in. And that all-in vision transformed Tesla into a trillion-dollar disruptor, a movement in vehicle engineering. He didn't stop there; every day he envisioned achieving newer milestones in space travel with SpaceX.

But here's the plot twist most founders miss. Having a killer vision is only the opening scene. The real movie begins when you marry it with an unabated focus on action. Musk or Sharma didn't just envision something; they remained loyal to their vision, and that indistinctive loyalty is what we call focus. A lot of startups fizzle out not because the idea sucked, but because they got distracted by every brand-new thing in the room.

Mindset Cue: Vision gives you direction; focus gives you momentum.

Clearly, the greats aren't the ones with a million ideas. They're the ones who follow one idea through the grind, glitches and glory.

Focus: The Unshakable Discipline

Vision steers. Focus executes.

Having a bold, game-changing vision? That's your startup's North Star. But what really fuels the rocket is your focus on everyday actions. You can sketch the grandest blueprint for world domination, but if your energy is scattered like a startup party popper, you'll end up building a sandcastle in a hurricane. Unlike a calm lake, the startup world is quite like a wild ocean full of waves – 'new trends', 'VC hype', 'glamorous opportunities', and the classic 'what if we also build this?' Without laser focus, even the most uncorrupted and undistracted sharp founders end up playing ping-pong everywhere and nowhere at once.

One great story is Zomato's. From humble restaurant reviews, their founders had a vivid vision to revolutionise the food landscape. However, they didn't launch delivery *and* grocery services overnight. They focused on reviews first, nailed a strong experience. After establishing its reputation as a reliable food-discovery platform, Zomato expanded into food delivery, cloud kitchens and grocery delivery, leveraging its brand and user base to fuel ongoing growth. Their growth wasn't random; it was a masterclass in timing and precision. One step at a time while staying true to their vision.

Here's the catch: when focus goes missing, execution turns into a hot mess. You start burning money in ten directions, your team becomes confused, and your product looks like several irrelevant, incongruous, odd pieces stitched together by a hyperactive builder. So if you're a founder in hustle mode, it is imperative to note that vision gets you in the arena, but it's focus that wins the match. Lock in, level up and leave the distractions for your competitors.

The Sweet Spot: Vision + Agility

A rigid vision is blind. Scattershot pivoting is chaotic. Real founders thrive in the middle – *anchored but agile.* Having laser focus matters, but not at the cost of becoming resistant to change. Some founders cling so tightly to their original plan that they ignore user feedback, market shifts, or fresh tech breakthroughs. True startup resilience lies in staying true to your mission while flexing when the world moves around you.

Mindset Cue: You don't build an empire by dancing from pole to pole; you build it by dominating one thing before you add more to the menu.

Think about Duolingo.[2] What began as a Carnegie Mellon research project with a bold promise – free language education powered by crowdsourced translation – snowballed into something much bigger. Duolingo spotted an opening – gamified, AI-driven lessons that feel less like homework and more like a game you can't put down. They didn't abandon their 'language education for all' vision. They amped it up with adaptive quizzes, streaks, certifications and clever monetisation. Today, millions turn to Duolingo because it tied its core vision with smart pivots. It became proof that agility fuels lasting success.

Agility isn't flipping your vision on its head; it's moulding that vision to fit real-world twists. Top founders know when to hold firm on their 'why' and when to tweak their 'how'. It's a dance. Plant your feet on purpose, but keep your arms free to catch opportunities.

The Mindset Shift

A killer vision sketches the big picture. Unwavering focus powers each step forward. The founders who triumph master both – dreaming boldly and executing with discipline. History shows that enduring companies combine a clear purpose, relentless focus and the agility to evolve without losing their core. Whether you're building the next global platform or a niche disruptor, winning means keeping your vision sharp, your execution precise, and your mind open to change.

Adopt this mindset, and you won't just survive startup hurdles, you'll build ventures that last, reshape industries, and leave a mark for years to come. Keep asking yourself. Is this aligned with our long-term mission? Is this action bringing us closer to our North Star?

Arc 2

Capital, Clarity and Control

7

The Money Mindset

Founders' Financial Vigil

EVERY FOUNDER KICKS OFF with spark and swagger, but without financial savvy, even the brightest ideas can fizzle. Many startups aren't crushed by bad products; they lose running out of money, misreading metrics, or chasing growth without a core revenue model to back it.

Behind every glamorous pitch deck and lofty ambition lies a less glamorous truth: **money matters**. Cultivating a financial compass helps a founder steer through uncertainty, seize opportunities, and survive inevitable storms.

Now that's not just about knowing your revenue from your rent; it's about mastering the money game. It means understanding where to put your capital, how to invest smartly, and how to future-proof your business for the long haul. Founders who ignore this often find themselves blindsided by surprise cash crunches, reckless spending habits, or business models built on shaky math. But founders who 'get' finance? They use numbers like a compass, making sharper decisions, scaling with confidence, and building startups that don't just survive, but thrive.

Mindset Cue: A sharp vision without financial vigilance is like a rocket without fuel – dazzling at launch, doomed in flight.

In this chapter, let's unpack the financial dynamics early-stage entrepreneurs must master. We shall cover cash flow rhythms, unit economics, profitability levers, runway and burn dynamics, forecasting rituals, risk management, vigil over metrics, and embedding a culture of financial awareness.

Cash Flow: The Heartbeat of a Startup

Cash flow is literal - money coming in versus money going out in real time. It's any startup's pulse. You can boast of skyrocketing user numbers, but if actual cash doesn't hit the account when bills arrive, you face a hard stop.

It's a revenue-versus-cash tussle. You might recognise revenue in accounting when an invoice is issued, but real liquidity only arrives when customers pay. A large contract is a burden if payments are delayed or held up by bureaucracy.

Mindset Cue: In finance, timing is everything. Salaries, rent, cloud bills, marketing spend – they don't wait for your next funding round.

Accounts receivable (AR) is the money owed to you. And accounts payable (AP) is the money you owe. The smart juggling between AR and AP is an art that founders must master to ensure that no hard stops appear suddenly to halt the operations.

Let's take WeWork, which once looked like the ultimate unicorn with growing trajectories, mission statements about elevating the work ecosystem, and a jaw-dropping $47 billion valuation.[1] The idea looked bold, but the money math was broken. They leased spaces for years and rented them for days. That's like paying year-long rent in the hopes that weekend guests will cover the bill. When occupancy didn't make it, cash didn't keep up, and expenses throttled.

Instead of fixing the fundamentals, WeWork doubled down on spending and global expansion, riding the VC funding rollercoaster straight into an IPO disaster in 2019. Significant losses, poor control and low cash reserves crashed the IPO and pushed founder Adam Neumann out. Hype can get you headlines, but without a solid cash strategy, even the coolest brand can crash hard.

Having said that, founders can definitely administer a couple of cash flow fixes to play seamlessly.

First, track cash like it's your lifeline. Forget hopeful projections that require a weekly ritual of reviewing actual cash in versus out. Build a three to six months rolling forecast and keep it updated with real numbers, not fantasised figures. Spot cash crunches early, long before your account is already gasping.

Second, master the art of inflows and outflows. Speed up your receivables. Acquire long-term customers or clients, offer early-payment perks, follow up like a pro, and negotiate smart terms to stretch out your payables. This balance keeps your runway longer and panic shorter.

Last, prepare for curveballs. Keep a non-negotiable buffer of three to four months of burn in the bank. And run regular 'what-if' drills. What if a big client delays payment? What if your burn spikes? What if the market season hits bad and customers don't turn? Have a plan before contingency.

Profitability: Beyond Just Revenue

Too many early-stage founders chase wild growth and eye-popping valuations, thinking profitability is an optional future luxury. Well, it's not. It's what keeps the lights on after the funding parties end.

Let's bust a popular startup myth: revenue ≠ profit. Yes, your monthly revenue rate (MRR) might look like a rockstar's Instagram follower count. But if your expenses are growing faster than your revenue, guess what? You're not winning, you're bleeding. You are burning more than you are earning. And that's where profitability dies.

So, what is profitability? In simple terms, it's the art of keeping more money than you spend. It's what makes your business sustainable. While revenue gets you applause, profitability buys you freedom. Freedom from chasing the next funding round, from burning out, and most importantly, to build on your own terms.

Let's break down a few foundational profitability terms that every founder, even the ones who hate spreadsheets or dashboards, must understand.

Gross Profit Margin

Gross profit margin tells you how much you're really making after delivering your product or service before you start paying your rent, salaries, or Wi-Fi subscriptions for the office. An indicator that tells you 'How Efficiently You Deliver'.

Simply,

Gross Profit or Gross Income = Net Revenue – Cost of Goods Sold

Gross Profit Margin = Gross Profit / Net Revenue

Let's say you run a D2C clothing brand. You sell a T-shirt for ₹1,000, but it costs you ₹400 to produce and ship it. That's ₹600 in gross profit or gross income. Your gross profit margin is 60 per cent. Nice!

Why does it matter? Well, if your gross margin is too low, scaling won't save you. It'll just burn you faster. A healthy margin is what gives you breathing space to pay people, market smart, and most importantly, reinvest.

Operating Profit Margin

Now that you've covered the cost of your product, let's account for all the overhead, like your team, software tools, office cookies, logistics, customer support, etc. The operating profit margin shows how much you're actually left with after running the whole operation.

Simply,

Operating Profit or Operating Income = Gross Profit – Operating Overheads or Expenses

Operating Profit Margin = Operating Profit / Net Revenue

That T-shirt still makes ₹600 in gross profit. But your design team, e-commerce platform, ad spends, and packaging logistics eat up ₹500. You're left with an operating profit of ₹100. That's a 10 per cent operating margin.

Why does it matter? This metric is the real health check. If it's low or negative, even a ₹10 crore revenue won't help much. You're spending more to run your business than you're earning from it, and that's a road to nowhere.

It's also referred to as EBIT (Earnings Before Interest and Taxes), which signifies that still non-operating costs are included in operating profits.

Net Profit Margin

Net profit is what's left in your pocket after interest payments, taxes and other expense adjustments. This is your *actual* profit.

Simply,
Net Profit / Net Income = Operating Income – Non-Operating Expenses and Adjustments
Net Profit Margin = Net Income / Net Revenue

For instance, your business earns ₹1 crore in revenue, ends up with ₹10 lakh in net income after all expenses. That's a 10 per cent net profit margin. It tells you that for every ₹100 earned, you retain ₹10.

Why does it matter? Net profit is what you can reinvest, save, or finally draw as salary. A high-revenue business with negative net profit is just a fancy money-burning machine.

A Few Tested Tips for Founders to Optimise Profitability

1. Don't just chase the topline. Revenue is attractive, but if margins suck, you're still broke.
2. Master unit economics. Know your levers. For each customer, track the customer acquisition cost (CAC), customer lifetime value (CLV), churn rate and margins. They impact profitability big time.
3. Cut noise, not value. Every rupee you spend should create leverage either through direct revenue, growth, efficiency, or brand trust.
4. Protect your pricing. Test pricing tiers, value-based pricing, and upsells; don't assume your first price is final. Over-discounting to acquire customers is a fast way to erode your margins.

5. Avoid vanity metrics. One million users sounds great. But how many are paying? Profitability shall always matter more than popularity.
6. Adopt the break-even mindset. Aim to break even at the unit level early, such as per user or per transaction, even if overall profitability comes later.
7. Optimise operations. Automate repetitive tasks, outsource non-core functions, and renegotiate supplier contracts.
8. Reinvest wisely. Channel early profits into high-ROI areas (product improvements, customer success) rather than vanity projects.

Profitability isn't some MBA jargon you can ignore until Series B. It's the DNA of a business that keeps it alive. You don't have to get there on Day 1. But you do need to keep your eye on it from the start. Track your margins. Manage your costs.

Mindset Cue: Building a real business isn't about how much you raise, it's about how much you make.

Take Zoho for instance. Instead of chasing VC cheques, it carved its way to profitability in a very frugal style.[2] Their disciplined, steady game with product, growth, finances and scale let them beat the best of the bests in the SaaS industry. Zoho's journey offers invaluable lessons for driven founders.

First, they rejected the 'burn-to-grow' VC-hyped mantra. Instead of chasing Silicon Valley's high-rent, high-burn lifestyle, Zoho built its tech HQ in Chennai and later even in rural Tamil Nadu. The saved funds went straight into product development, not beanbags or Meta-like office decor!

Second, they chose product-led growth over paid ads. Zoho never burned VC money on Google or Facebook campaigns. They let the product speak for itself. Happy users spread the word, creating organic buzz and loyal fans. Their smart planning made customer acquisition almost free – powered by trust, not spending.

Third, Zoho chose a no-debt, no-dilution, no-drama mindset. They relied on their unit economics and net margins to grow and scale. Zoho didn't just say no to VC; they said no to unnecessary loans, fancy acquisitions and external pressure to scale faster than sanity would allow. That meant they kept ownership, stayed profitable, and controlled their own road map – an epic illustration of how bootstrapped ventures must build.

Lastly, Zoho kept a close watch on its cash flows, defined clear success metrics, built a long-term plan, and led a simple, profitable expansion. Zoho proved that you can build a global brand, earn billions in revenue, and do it all while owning your company and staying debt-free.

Zoho's story illustrates a golden rule. *You don't have to burn cash to build value.*

Runway and Burn Rate: The Clock and the Flame

After you've understood cash flow and taken a deep breath with profitability, it's time to look at the two metrics that actually decide how long your startup can breathe at all – runway and burn rate.

Simply, burn rate means how fast you're *spending* your cash, and runway means how much *time* you have left before that cash is gone.

These aren't glamorous terms. No one boasts about them on founder panels or startup reels. But behind every healthy, scalable company is a founder who not only tracks these two numbers but also respects them as laws of startup mechanics.

Burn rate is the amount of *net cash* your startup spends every month.

Simply,

Net Burn = Monthly Cash Outflow – Monthly Cash Inflow

It tells you how fast your money is melting! This spend is not just salaries. It's rent, tools, freelancers, coffee, chai, last-minute Adobe license upgrades, and that one AI tool you subscribed to but never used.

Mindset Cue: If cash is your fuel, burn rate is your mileage. You can burn slow and stay longer in the game. Or burn hot and look cool, right before the crash.

High burn isn't always bad. If you're investing in customer acquisition and your unit economics are healthy, you're fuelling growth. But if your LTV/CAC looks like a bad joke and your burn is on fire, it clearly means you're not scaling, you're just burning money for warmth.

Let's say a D2C brand, GrabEthnic, is spending ₹15 lakh per month on marketing, team and operations. However, it's only pulling in ₹8 lakh in gross profit per month. That means its net burn is ₹7 lakh per month. If they don't increase margins, pull back on spend, or boost revenue, they'll run out of cash before they run out of product shots for Instagram!

So yes, the flame is on; the burn is manageable until you run out of fuel. And this 'until', this countdown clock is your runway. It reflects how many months your startup has left before it reaches a flatline, assuming no significant change in burn rate or revenue.

Simply,
Runway (in months) = Current Cash / Monthly Burn Rate

Say, you've got ₹1 crore in the bank. Your net burn is ₹20 lakh a month. Your standing runway (not projected) is five months.

Now, let's say for a key partnership, you have to hire additional resources and kick off new development, spiking your burn. Your new burn becomes ₹35 lakh. Suddenly, the current runway drops to three months. That small shift can trigger a domino effect of urgent decisions, including scrambling for funds, cutting experimental projects, pausing pipeline hires, or even layoffs.

Runway isn't just about survival; it's about timing. The shorter your runway, the less time you've got to fix the track. It wrecks your power to negotiate with investors, banks or clients, your ability to afford risky pivots, your freedom to choose the pace and your inner cognitive balance. You cannot expect to levitate healthy funds with a ticking clock and sweaty palms.

So, you've got five months of runway. Not five years. Not 'let's see how it goes'. Just five months. This number is not a prediction. It's a fact. The kind of fact that separates dreamers from doers.

Many early-stage founders treat runway like that one reality locker you never open because you're afraid of what's inside. But ignorance isn't bliss. It's impending bankruptcy. Knowing your runway sets your hiring pace. It decides whether you fundraise or survive on your own funds. It forces you to eliminate vanity features and be ruthless about distractions.

Runway isn't a one-time tattoo that's etched once, never reworked. A founder keeps vigilance on this one metric after every significant dynamism in the finances of the company. You might be relaxed, thinking, 'Oh, I have six months' easy cash in the bank account and yet more to come.' But unexpectedly, expenses creep, clients delay, experiments collapse, and suddenly your six-month cushion is halved. Some wait till panic hour to act, thinking they'll 'figure it out' later. Well, you might not get that luxury of time. When desperation sets in, it wipes away clarity. And let's not forget the blind optimism of ignoring what-ifs, such as delayed funding or a spike in CAC. Hope isn't a strategy. Runway math needs realism.

For instance, take FabbNow, a fashion-tech startup from Indore. They raised ₹40 lakh in pre-seed funding, built a beautiful website, opened micro-warehouses in three cities, hired content creators, and ran influencer campaigns that positioned them as the next big thing. But the numbers present a sobering reality.

Mindset Cue: Every startup faces a unique interplay of burn, revenue and runway, and it's the founder's decisions that tip the scale towards survival or struggle.

They were burning ₹7 lakh a month.
Revenue? Barely ₹1 lakh a month.
Net Burn? Approximately ₹6 lakh a month.
Runway? Less than 7 months.

They chose to scale in three cities without validating even in one. With no revenue forecast and meagre funds, they adopted a 'let us look like the next big thing' approach. But reality hits hard. With no significant revenue growth, naive optimism and unprojected burn rates, they soon fell short of the fuel to run. By the time they tried to raise more, it was too late. Investors backed off. The founders had no cash and no time. They didn't fail because of the product. They failed because they didn't respect the runway.

Mindset Cue: Don't spend like a unicorn when you haven't even become a pony.

A founder with nine months of runway thinks differently from one with two months of runway. One builds leverage. The other begs.

Five-Pointer Runway Rituals

Runway is about time discipline, and with revenue-burning dynamics, runway struggle is not a crime for founders. All one needs to master is the art of managing the runway until the track is fixed. So when the runway is imminent, I advise founders to employ the following five-point approach to turn the remaining months into startup fuel rather than a startup funeral.

Point 1: Reduce burn, regulate run. Look at every burn item smartly. Do you really need a 20-person hierarchical marketing team, or can you co-play some more roles till your finances ease dedicated hires? Can your designer survive without Figma Pro? Will the world end if you delay that offsite in Bali? How about that flashy feature that doesn't add to your product's core functionality? Trim the fat. Keep the muscle.

Point 2: Boost revenue. Even if it's ugly, sell what you can, even if it's not your dream product yet. Run paid webinars. Offer one-on-one consults. Do workshops. Hustle. Revenue buys time. Time buys better decisions.

Point 3: Stretch your cash with smart timing. Collect customer payments faster. Delay vendor payments politely. Avoid locking cash in annual deals unless they save big. This isn't being stingy. It's called founder yoga – flexibility saves lives.

Point 4: Fundraise before you look desperate. No one gives you money when you're already gasping. Start conversations when you have six to nine months of runway left. You negotiate more effectively with a full stomach and a calm demeanour. Desperation repels money. Confidence attracts it.

Point 5: Track runway monthly, religiously. Make it a ritual. Open your bank balance, calculate burn and update your runway. Even a simple Excel sheet can save you ₹5 lakh worth of stupidity. Startups don't die in boardrooms. They die in dashboards no one updated.

The above approach is to avoid any impending situation. To stay sane and avoid crying over financial issues, founders are advised to follow these runway rituals.

> **Mindset Cue: You don't hit contingency overnight; it builds quietly, then strikes hard. Thus, act proactively.**

Build a rolling three- to six-month forecast, and update it every few weeks to stay financially alert. Use scenario planning for best, base, and worst cases to prepare smart responses before trouble hits. Set runway triggers so you act early, and not in panic. Hire like a bootstrapped ninja. Focus on only what's essential, and outsource the rest. Boost short-term revenue through pilots or referrals, but watch your unit economics. And when the runway tightens, be transparent with your core team. It builds trust and often sparks creative fixes you didn't see coming.

Take Freshworks for instance. The Chennai-born SaaS venture began keeping its team size under 50, avoided bloated marketing spends by prioritising product-led growth via free tiers that converted organically, and tightly managed burn. Revenue came from tiered upgrades like Freshdesk, Freshsales, etc. They kept burn rate low, focused on retention, and built a product people wanted to return to, stretching runway over a decade to $500M+ ARR while staying capital-efficient and investor-friendly.

As founders, your job isn't just to build a great aircraft. It's to keep that vessel in the air with enough altitude (cash), fuel (revenue), and a reliable, up-to-date map (financial forecast). You don't need a finance degree. You need discipline, vigilance and a willingness to ask hard questions early. So before your next funding call or hiring spree, check your gauge. Is your runway long enough? Or are you flying to fall eventually?

The Mindset Shift

Ultimately, securing funds or launching a novel product matters. But a founder's crucial test lies in mastering the basics that keep the engine running. Vision sets the direction. Financial vigilance keeps the ship afloat. As a founder, you monitor your cash flow, margins, burn rate and runway as if your life depends on it, because it does. Treat your metrics as your compass. Review your numbers periodically. Map and plan for every scenario. Stay grounded in facts, not optimism. In the startup world, the ideas that survive are built on discipline, clarity and enough runway to finish the race.

8

The Team Mindset

Building a High-Octane Squad

A STARTUP IS AS good as its founders, and founders are as good as their team. A startup's true superpower isn't the code, the product, or the fancy pitch; it's the people that bring it all to life. Before product-market fit, and before Series A cheques arrive, your team is both your runway and your parachute. In a scrappy, early-stage, resource-lean environment, far beyond just employees, your first hires are culture-setters, problem-solvers, validators and the propellers that drive every pivot. Get the team wrong, and you'll be firefighting personnel issues instead of pivoting, growing or scaling impact. Get it right, and you'll unlock innovation, velocity and grit in action.

As a founder, your most important job is to build, nurture and lead a squad that thrives under uncertainty. That means more than checking résumés. It means creating a place where people feel trusted, empowered, and excited to tackle tomorrow's challenges today. In this chapter, we'll unpack how to spot and bring on the right players, shape a culture that propels performance, and lead in a way that keeps your people inspired and aligned for the long haul.

The Hiring Process: Selecting the Right People

One of the biggest mistakes early-stage founders make is hiring too quickly, sometimes carelessly prioritising skills over cultural fit or proximity over potential. While expertise is vital, someone who can't adapt or doesn't thrive in a fast-moving environment can stall your progress and unsettle your team. Hiring isn't simply transactional. It's foundational. Imagine you bring on a world-class coder who craves structure, monthly sprints and clear road maps, but your startup pivots weekly and thrives on chaos. That mismatch can grind teams to a halt.

Startups face constant uncertainty and high stakes, so it's crucial to recruit people who embrace ambiguity, take full ownership, and act without waiting for instructions. A smart hiring strategy weighs three elements equally – skills, mindset and cultural fit to fuel sustained growth.

Now the question here is: how does a founder spot his 'right' people? We can't procrastinate on the issue of finding and hiring a team, waiting for the perfect squad. As the same time, it can't be a desperate hire-fire-hire adventure. This requires a stable, aware and mature mindset from the founder. Top candidates aren't only after big paycheques. They seek meaningful work, purpose that resonates, clear growth paths and a culture that mirrors their values and aspirations.

As a founder, you are not the only one behind the best talent; several are. Thus, your team-building approach must stand out to attract the superheroes. Here is how you can hit that cord right:

Mindset Cue: When a founder's proposal meets a talent's aspiration, momentum becomes unstoppable.

1. Assess grit before grades. Look for spark and drive. People who dive in, ask 'Why not?' and roll up their sleeves. Don't look for the right aptitude but the right attitude. You can teach tools, you can't teach passion. Watch for those who own problems rather than passing them off. A team of eager learners becomes your greatest multiplier. That doesn't mean ruling out skills, but assessing 'the right' personality first.
2. Purpose should pull. Paint a vivid picture of your 'why'. Share quick success stories and growth moments so talent feels compelled to join your cause. When candidates see themselves in your story, they'll jump at the chance to join. A shared vision turns hires into true believers.
3. Run curveball screening. In interviews, ditch generic questions and hit candidates with real-world curveballs: 'Our app crashed, what's your first move?'; 'A high-value client got a better price deal from a freelancer, how do

you still retain it?'; 'A major investor pulled out. How do you rally the team?' Watch who leaps forward with a plan, not who freezes. Pay attention to their solution and communication. Clear ideas today mean fewer misfires tomorrow. This approach weeds out bystanders and surface role owners.

4. Pack and pitch long-haul perks. Offer more than money, like day-one equity, learning stipends, surprise bonuses, flexible hours, and so on. Tailor perks smartly to fuel curiosity and reward milestones that matter. These thoughtful extras make your startup feel like more than a job; it becomes an adventure. Small gestures spark lasting loyalty. When you mirror your team's aspirations, their growth, autonomy and impact, they'll grab your offer faster than any recruiter can ping them. Founders often panic-hire, offering perks, titles and leniency to lock in talent before a competitor does. But desperation hires dilute performance. Never trade clear outcomes for quick onboardings.
5. Build lean as far as possible. Hire only when a missing skill truly blocks your path. A tight crew moves faster, talks less, and delivers more. Fewer hands mean clearer roles and stronger ownership. When each hire counts, every person steps up.

The Duolingo Team

Duolingo's hiring genesis feels more like assembling a dream team of language lovers than ticking off a skills checklist.[1] From the start, founders Luis von Ahn and Severin Hacker looked for engineers who could build robust apps, linguists who got a kick out of tricky grammar twists, and designers who knew how to turn learning into a game. But above all, they wanted people who believed everyone deserves free access to language education. Skills mattered. But spirit mattered more.

Duolingo made hiring fun. Candidates joined playful 'teach-a-phrase' rounds like explaining 'My penguin wears pyjamas'.[2]

The goal wasn't a perfect résumé; it was to spot people who could take feedback, think creatively, and bring real joy to learning.

Every hire was mission-first. Candidates had to believe that learning a language could build business and, more importantly, create a lasting impact. This wasn't about joining in. It was about showing up for a cause. They kept the team lean as well. Every new hire wore multiple hats. One day, tweaking an app feature, the next day sketching mascot ideas or testing user flows. Ideas travelled fast and so did decisions. This tight crew could ship updates fast. Launch on Tuesday, check user reactions on Wednesday, and tweak again by Thursday.

Above all, Duolingo hired for the long haul. Interviews tested adaptability with questions like 'How would you teach someone a word they've never heard?' and teamwork tasks, such as 'Pair up with a linguist and brainstorm together'. They weren't just filling seats. They were building a squad ready to grow with the platform, adding new languages and even AI tutors down the road.

They bet on purpose. They won with people. And that's how a tiny, mission-led team taught millions to say hello in more than 40 languages and build a unicorn at a valuation of over $5 billion.

Culture: The Subtle Gear

A startup's culture isn't about free snacks, bean bag chairs, Insta-ready office spaces or other vanities. It's the invisible DNA that guides how your team collaborates, learns and stays resilient when the going gets tough. A healthy culture fuels creativity and commitment. A toxic one leads to rapid burnout and early exits. As you begin to build your startup, culture isn't cooked overnight but hand-built personally by founders over a period. As founders, you set the tone in every Slack message, every board-room decision or discussion. Every communication and action signals what truly matters.

Mindset Cue: Culture isn't copied; it's hand-coded by its founders. It's the mirror of its founder's personality and choices.

After assessing and assimilating the culture playbooks of over a hundred global startups, I've capsuled the most winning approaches as **VIBES**, a practical, founder-ready framework to build and sustain a high-voltage startup culture.

'V' stands for *Values in Action.* Instead of pinning core values on a slide deck, embed them in how you hire, review and reward. If 'ownership' is a value, publicly admit to mistakes. If you champion 'customer obsession', jump on a support call once in a while. More things are caught than taught. As a founder, you are always observed and you always inspire.

'I' stands for *Invoke Transparent Voices.* Create low-barrier channels such as anonymous feedback forms, weekly 'Ask Us Anything (AMA)' sessions, open virtual office hours, etc. so ideas and concerns flow freely and solutions emerge fast.

'B' stands for *Back Autonomy with Accountability.* Give squads real decision-making power and clear end goals. When people feel full ownership of their work, they innovate faster and take accountability seriously.

'E' stands for *Encourage Learning.* Fuel upskilling and up-learning by hosting 'lunch and learn' workshops, running mini-hackathons and peer-to-peer skill-sharing breakouts. A learning-first mindset keeps your team agile and ahead of industry shifts.

'S' stands for *Snooze to Soar.* Work with fire, but don't forget to recharge. Enforce 'no-meeting' days, encourage unplugged weekends, and offer mental-health resources. A refreshed team outperforms one that is running on fumes.

Nail the VIBES framework, and you'll transform your startup from a collection of individuals into a cohesive engine of creativity and resilience. Because in the grind of day-to-day hustle, it's your people who turn obstacles into opportunities and ideas into impact.

Paytm stands as a textbook example of relentless culture. When Paytm burst onto the scene, it didn't just digitise wallets; it rewired the entire DNA of financial services in India. Forget slow-moving banks bound by boardroom approvals. Paytm built a 'fail fast, learn faster' playground where experimentation was the norm, not the exception. Several highly conducive practices contributed to supercharging its team and culture.

First, they smashed the myth that finance and agility don't gel together. Small cross-functional squads at Paytm were handed the ownership of their own features. Front-end engineers, UX designers, data analysts, even compliance leads each empowered to prototype, A/B test, and launch within days. Real-time user feedback flowed straight back into their sprint cycles, so every glitch or friction point became a chance to iterate. The result? Paytm rolled out new offerings from mobile recharges to instant small-ticket loans at a pace that left legacy banking, non-banking and other fintech players scrambling to catch up.

Second, 'autonomy with accountability' wasn't just an institutional jingle. It became their operating model. Instead of one-size-fits-all, top-down memos from the C-suite, ideas bubbled up from the ground. Got a bold idea for wealth management on the app? Pitch it. Build a quick demo. If metrics showed promise, you got a budget to scale. If not, you shelved it. No blame, just insight. That decentralised decision-making supercharged creativity and kept bureaucracy at bay.

Third, Paytm invested relentlessly in continuous learning. From lunchtime 'tech-hack' meetups to monthly leadership workshops, they made sure every 'Paytmite' could sharpen skills and swap knowledge. When India's digital infrastructure shifted, Paytm's teams were already well versed in the latest APIs, security protocols and customer-behaviour analytics, ready to pivot on a dime.

Finally, they treated calculated risks as tuition rather than punishment. Every 'failure' underpinned a retrospective that distilled learnings, updated playbooks, and fuelled the next experiment. This fearless, feedback-driven culture built confidence, resilience and deep alignment around a shared vision to democratise financial services for hundreds of millions of Indians.

By integrating decentralisation, rapid prototyping, and empowered teams across all layers of its organisation, Paytm became more than a payment app. It became a living case study in how a startup can stay relentlessly innovative at scale.

ESOP: The Founders' Secret Weapon

If you want people to build like owners, give them ownership. As simple as that!

In the early days of a startup, you're asking people to take a bet on you – often at a lower salary, with longer hours and a high degree of uncertainty. What's the best way to make that risk feel worthwhile? Give them skin in the game. That's what employee stock ownership plans (ESOPs) are meant to do. Not just to compensate, but to commit.

Early-stage startups often can't compete with corporate paycheques, but they can offer something far more powerful: *ownership*. An ESOP is not just compensation; it's a tool for alignment, trust, and long-term loyalty. It turns employees into stakeholders and distributes ownership across the shoulders.

A well-designed ESOP makes employees co-owners in the company's growth. Begin with a clear structure. For instance, a four-year vesting period with a one-year cliff is a good standard. *We'll get into ESOP details in the upcoming chapter –* 'The Equity Mindset'.

What really unlocks the power of ESOP is awareness and transparency. Many employees don't fully understand what equity means, so founders must explain the mechanics, potential upside, and timing in real, tangible terms.

Let's take Flipkart, one of India's landmark ESOP success stories.[3] Few Indian startups have created more wealth for employees than Flipkart. In 2018, when Walmart acquired Flipkart for $16 billion, it triggered one of India's largest ESOP liquidation events. More than $500 million (₹3,500 crore) was distributed to Flipkart employees through share buybacks. From senior executives and mid-level managers to early engineers and product teams, hundreds of employees benefitted from this massive exit. Some early hires reportedly received multi-crore payouts, which forever changed the Indian startup ecosystem's view of ESOPs as a credible path to wealth creation.

Mindset Cue: When people feel like they truly own a piece of what they're building, they stop working for a company and start building a legacy.

What made Flipkart's ESOP journey so effective wasn't just the massive exit but the consistent culture of equity. The founders, Sachin and Binny Bansal, strongly believed in distributing ownership early and often. As Flipkart scaled, it continued to expand the ESOP pool and offer top-ups during fundraising rounds, ensuring contributors at every level had a meaningful stake. They also introduced buyback programmes before the Walmart exit, allowing some employees to unlock value early. This demonstrates that even pre-exit liquidity is attainable with the right planning.

Founders can stick to the following principles to strike a win-win proposition while hiring in the early stage, especially:

- Be generous early. Offer ESOPs, not just to CXOs but to early product, ops and tech hires who shape the foundation.
- Educate consistently. Don't assume people understand how equity works. Walk them through scenarios during onboarding and funding rounds.
- Don't just give out ESOPs, explain them. Clarity builds trust. Use visuals, examples and real-time value updates.
- Create a real upside. Secondary sales or buybacks send a strong message of trust and reward. Liquidity signals to your team that their patience is valued.
- Update pools as you grow. Tie option pool expansions with new milestones and make sure early employees don't get diluted unfairly.

Stories like that of Flipkart prove that ESOPs are not just theoretical wealth. They can change lives. They showed India's startup workforce that betting on an early-stage venture could create generational wealth. As a founder, when you treat equity as a serious promise instead of a vague bonus, you don't just retain talent. Instead, you ignite ownership. And that can become your biggest competitive edge.

The Co-Founders' Cohesion: Unity at the Top

Co-founders are the living pillars of your startup. Their bond and shared mindset set the tone for every hire, decision and pivot that follows. While employee dynamics can be managed through HR policies, co-founder dynamics demand deliberate attention to role clarity, mutual trust and emotional resilience. This forms the bedrock of a team that won't splinter under pressure.

However, startups present a spectrum of challenges, and co-founders are tested for resilience across a variety of contexts. To help founders, I have listed five psychological pitfalls that can fracture co-founder unity, along with simple rituals to maintain cohesion.

Mindset Cue: Beyond code and capital, a startup is fundamentally built on the trust, clarity and the emotional stamina of its leaders.

First, it's the ego tug-of-war. When personal identity and roles collide, debates become battles. Each co-founder needs a decision charter that maps who owns what choices and when joint input is required. This shifts disputes from 'you versus me' to 'role versus role', defusing personal pride and ensuring decisions stay productive.

Second, the silent resentment loop. Unspoken expectations breed hidden frustration. A monthly mutual check-in with two self-prompts – *what did I appreciate this month,* and *what can we handle better next time?* – turns vague annoyances into clear feedback, preventing small slights from growing into trust-eroding grudges.

Third, it's the avoidance trap. At times, postponed equity talks or vision debates become emotional debt when left unaddressed. Schedule quarterly 'hard talks' as structured conversations on ownership, commitment and goals so that difficult topics are resolved on mutual terms, not under crisis or pressure.

Fourth, pressure breaks partnerships. High stress hijacks calm thinking and triggers blame. A simple ten-minute daily rhythm, say a morning goal sync and an evening emotional download, serves as self-regulation. Clearly naming frustrations and aligning priorities now and then helps founders stay clear-headed and prevents reactive fallout.

Lastly, the comparison spiral. Measuring success against peers can fuel impostor syndrome. Combat this with a weekly 'three wins' ritual, noting one achievement for product, team and personal growth each. This practice reframes progress as steady momentum, not endless benchmarking, and keeps focus on your own journey.

A rock-solid co-founder bond is the bedrock of any lasting venture. Get that foundation right, and the rest of the team will stand firm, grow fast and weather any storm.

Few failures illustrate leadership misalignment as clearly as Quibi. Despite a staggering net funding, it folded in just six months. Why? Misalignment. Founder A, Jeffrey Katzenberg, pursued major content; Founder B, Meg Whitman, prioritised streamlined operations. Rather than combining their strengths, they worked in comfortable isolation from each other. Eventually, fast decisions became slow arguments, pivots were delayed, and user traction collapsed. With fewer than 5,00,000 subscribers against a 7 million target, Quibi demonstrated that capital doesn't compensate for a fractured leadership core.

Startups don't fail as much because of bad ideas as they falter when steering co-founders lose sync. A strong co-founder dynamic is built with clarity, honesty and a rhythm of mutual respect. Beyond contracts, the real code of conduct lies in how you talk when you disagree, how you show up when it's hard, and how you remind each other why you started together in the first place.

The Zerodha Team

Before we move to the next chapter, I can't resist discussing Zerodha, a unicorn that nailed team building like no other. Long before they upended India's brokerage industry, co-founders Nikhil and Nithin Kamath hired friends and ex-colleagues who believed in zero-commission trading as much as they did.[4] They didn't chase pedigrees. They chased commitment to experimentation, transparency and customer obsession. That tight-knit squad built a platform that now handles billions of dollars in trades, simply because everyone on the team felt a shared ownership in its success (and its failures).

Addressing early traders on his comparatively crude platform, Nithin once said, 'What makes or breaks a business is the people working.'[5]

Zerodha built its team in a relentlessly lean, mission-first style. Here is what worked for them.

First, when Nithin and Nikhil Kamath launched Zerodha in 2010, their 'team' was more of a seven-person joint family: Nikhil handled trading and risk management; Venu took care of compliance and operations; Hanan ran customer support; Sameer oversaw dealing; Parwez led sales; Sundar managed administration; and Nithin did everything else. Fast-forward to 16 million customers, and it's still roughly a thousand people. Remarkably, Zerodha managed to serve 10x more customers with the *same* headcount. That's proof that scaling via people count isn't always the answer.

Second, rather than hiring 'fintech pedigree', Zerodha sought integrity, learning agility and cultural fit. As of today, a 36-person core tech force, with only 10 per cent from financial services backgrounds, is in operation at Zerodha. Hiring largely measures ownership and aptitude, not alma mater. Just five new tech hires in four years is the proof of a deep bench strength and team cohesion. This lean approach forced autonomy: founders relinquished 'how' in favour of 'what', trusting a lean tech team that punched above its weight.

Third, Zerodha maintains a deliberately flat organisational structure that minimises layers and promotes autonomy among its roughly 1,000 employees, with key leaders like the CEO, CTO and COO handling core functions rather than rigid reporting chains. Deep hierarchies are avoided while founders remain highly accessible, and 'fire drills' help identify natural leaders during crises without formal titles dominating. No individual revenue targets exist – instead, the team unites around collective profitability, long-term sustainability, and customer trust as guiding principles.

Lastly, Zerodha mastered retention through mission, not money. 'Those who join for money will leave for more money,' says Nithin Kamath. Zerodha walks the talk by allocating significant percentage of annual profits to bonuses and salary hikes, running ESOP buybacks to offer fair exits, and keeping hiring razor-focused to preserve team stickiness.

The Mindset Shift

A startup's real strength isn't just its product. It's the people behind it. The right team turns ideas into action, adapts when things change, and pushes through rough patches. Founders need to hire with purpose and clarity. Every hire should echo the startup's long-term vision. Skills matter, but ownership, trust and drive matter more. A strong team and robust culture spark problem-solving, encourage initiative, and build momentum. In the end, it's not the product that wins the market. It's the people who build, believe and back it every single day.

9

The Equity Mindset

Managing the Cap Table Without Drama

MORE THAN THE NUMBERS on a spreadsheet, equity is the narrative of trust, sweat and strategic trade-offs that shape a startup's ownership structure. When you carve your company into shares, you're not just divvying up ownership. You are making promises – to co-founders who've poured in vision, to early hires who've burned the midnight oil, and to investors who've bet on your grit. Treat those promises casually, and you'll sow mistrust, misalignment and morale meltdowns just when unity matters most.

At its simplest, *equity* is a slice of the ownership pie, measured in shares instead of slices. The *cap table* (short for 'capitalisation table') is the ledger that tracks who owns what percentage. Founders, early employees, investors, promoters and advisory partners are all listed in neat columns. *Dilution* happens when you add more slices to the pie. Your piece shrinks on paper, but ideally, the overall pie grows bigger. And *ESOPs* are the special slices you reserve to reward team members, turning hired hands into co-owners.

Mastering the Equity Mindset means seeing these terms not for the sake of dry accounting, but as living tools for alignment and motivation. This chapter helps founders perceive equity as currency and commitment, without letting drama dilute the dream.

The Cap Table Conundrum

Before term sheets and ESOP pools, before headlines about 'raising a round', there's a table you build – the cap table that maps who owns how much of your company. It measures ownership by equity shares. Sounds like accounting? It's not. Let's get one thing straight. Equity isn't just math, it's strategy. It's the combined narrative of trust, sweat, stakes and strategic trade-offs.

Most first-time founders don't realise this early enough. They see percentages, 5 per cent, 20 per cent, 40 per cent, and think the game is fair as long as everyone has 'some skin in the game'. But ownership isn't just what's written on paper.

It's what people believe they've earned and what value you believe they can bring to the table. And mismanaging that belief can spark years of silent resentment or messy conflict of interests.

In the early stages, equity gets split like pizza slices. The process is as casual as 'we're all friends, let's divide it equally'. Imagine a founding duo. They split the equity 50/50 because it felt fair. But over time, one builds the product, hires the team, and pitches to VCs, while the other occasionally dials in. Now what? Technically, they're equals. Functionally, not so much. That's where the 'Cap Table Conundrum' begins, not because of greed, but because the psychology of ownership wasn't acknowledged from the start.

Mindset Cue: Perceived ownership drives behaviour more than actual shareholding. When someone feels like a 5 per cent co-founder, even with 20 per cent on paper, your team is already misaligned.

To navigate this smartly, founders need a mindset shift. As a founder, one must run a **SAFE** check ritual quarterly to ensure a stable, aligned, and future-proof ownership structure for the business.

'S' stands for *Scan the Stakes*. Know the exact equity you and others hold today. Don't rely on memory. Open the spreadsheet and face the math.

'A' stands for *Assess Future Scenarios.* Question what happens if we raise another round or onboard three key hires. Model out dilution now, not during the pitch.

'F' stands for *Foster Candid Talks.* Sit with your co-founders. Is everyone still functionally aligned with what they own? Misalignment brews silently.

'E' stands for *Eliminate Unjust Giveaways.* Avoid gifting big chunks to non-core hires or advisors too early. Equity is the stickiest thing to undo. Treat it like gold.

A SAFE cap table reflects stakeholder alignment, strategic foresight, founder sanity, and the startup's stability.

S.A.F.E. Check for Cap Table Management

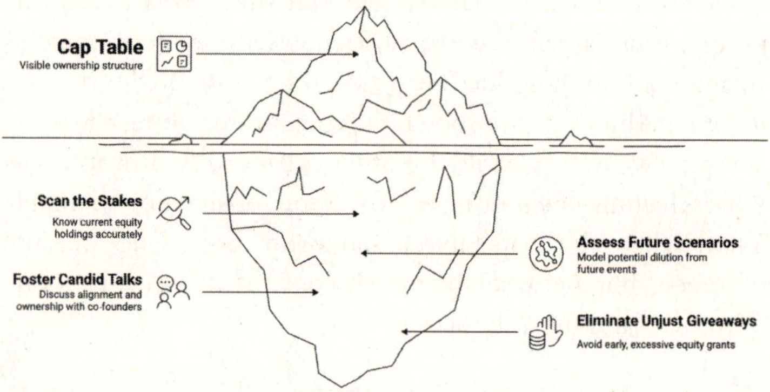

The sooner you see equity as a living agreement, the more control you'll keep over your startup's future. Treat your cap table like a sacred record. In startups, ownership isn't just about shares. It's about power, trust and destiny.

Ownership Dilution: Value over Percentage

At its core, a cap table reflects the ownership division that evolves as newer stakeholders join the table. As your startup grows and raises money, that table swells. Every funding round, every hire, every advisor deal affects the cap table, and if you're not paying attention, you might wake up owning a lot less than you imagined. As the table evolves with new stakeholders joining, ownership dilution hits in.

Founders often flinch at the word *dilution,* like it's a death sentence. 'I had 80 per cent, now I only own 42 per cent,' they lament. But here's the mindset shift. Perceiving dilution as decay is immaturity. As you grow, you realise it actually buys you direction.

> **Mindset Cue: More than a trophy to preserve, equity is a tool to trade for growth.**

You'd rather own 10 per cent of a ₹1,000 crore company than 80 per cent of a ₹1 crore company. Founders who cling to large slices often end up owning big pieces of a stalled pie. But those who treat equity like a catalyst unlock value that far exceeds their share shrinkage. Holding onto too much equity might feel like control, but it can quietly choke your growth. It can block capital, talent and partnerships when they matter most.

Now, that doesn't mean the percentage of founders' stakes doesn't hold any merit. It does. It straightaway determines the control and authority to steer the business. And that's why a founder is expected to make well-calculated choices of trading the control for value. The truth? Equity hoarding rarely scales companies. Value creation does.

Every funding round, ESOP grant, or equity partnership that triggers dilution should answer a simple question: *will this move compound our momentum*? When done right, dilution is a sure leverage, not a sacrifice. You are strategically trading a chip of control for exponential outcomes. A move that takes you from being a local player to being a market leader, or from MVP to industry gold standard.

Here's a simple, founder-tested decision filter you can use: the **3× Multiplier Rule**. Ask: 'Will giving up this bit of equity create at least 3× value in revenue, product strength, market reach, or speed?' If yes, it's your cap table driving compounding returns, not dilution.

It's a move from linear thinking to exponential play. It's not about giving up power, but unlocking acceleration. Instead of fearing dilution, real founders master it.

See how Razorpay weaponised equity play.[1] In 2014, while most fintechs were busy guarding their cap tables like family gold, Razorpay's founders, Harshil Mathur and Shashank Kumar, leaned into the founder-market fit and bet big. They knew the payment pain of Indian startups firsthand, and they knew that solving it at scale required speed, not stinginess.

So, they raised. And diluted. Early and often. Critics called it reckless. But every round bought them world-class talent, richer features and lightning-fast growth. Meanwhile, the bootstrapped 'equity protectors' stayed lean too long and missed the wave. Razorpay? They went from two guys and a prototype to a unicorn with 30 per cent market share in just six years.[2]

Smart dilution is a launchpad. But not every founder practises and masters it equally well.

Unlike Razorpay, Dunzo is altogether a different case of smart dilution. Instead of chasing fat funding rounds, Dunzo mastered the art of just enough. Between 2016 and 2018, they raised multiple bridging micro rounds. Rather than a desperate move, it served as a deliberate strategy to stretch the runway without losing grip. Each round unlocked proof points such as improved delivery operations, tighter product loops and market learnings, all without bloating the cap table or burning out. While others traded giant cheques for chaos, Dunzo played the long game. They did not dilute in panic. They diluted with purpose.

The ESOP Equation: Equity Without Envy

Building momentum through dilution is only half the battle. The other half is ensuring your team feels that momentum in their own bank of promise, especially the early hires who carry you through the tough tracks. That's where ESOPs kick in as your loyalty lever, transforming a 'just a job' attitude into 'owning the mission'. They turn paycheques into pay-offs, weaving ownership and long-term commitment into every engineer, designer and marketer's DNA. At its core, an ESOP grants rights to buy shares at a fixed price down the road, so your team wakes up every morning knowing they own a piece of the dream.

Especially in an early-stage startup, cash is tight, and talent is everything. ESOPs flip the script, offering upside instead of a fat salary. They bind ambitious hires to your mission, converting paycheque-pushers into long-term believers. More than perks, they forge a shared destiny; they hustle harder, innovate smarter, and stay longer. This mindset of treating ESOPs not as HR glitter but as strategic currency is what separates teams that scale from those that stall.

Let's unwind a few basics around ESOPs to keep things real. At its simplest, ESOP signifies a *pool of shares* you reserve for employees, advisors and early believers. Instead of cash bonuses, you grant *options* – the right to buy shares later at today's *strike price* (the set price per share at grant date) after a *vesting period* (commonly four years with a one-year 'cliff' after which the vested options can be exercised to convert into shares). Thus your team becomes co-owners with skin in the game.

But ESOPs can backfire if not administered with clarity and transparency. Hand out generous slices without context and reasoning, and you spark equity envy to find your people gossiping: 'Why did she get 2 per cent and I only got 0.2 per cent?' Worse, options can appear illusory if vesting schedules and price mechanics remain mysteries. Your early engineer might see his options vesting over four years, but if he doesn't understand strike prices or liquidity events, that 'ownership' never translates into real value. That's where clarity at ESOP allocation gets vital.

Smart founders avoid ESOP chaos by keeping things clear from Day 1. Simplicity wins over secrecy. Share a one-pager that explains vesting, exercise windows and exit scenarios in plain words, not legal jargon. Say it like this: 'If we hit a ₹500 crore exit, your 0.5 per cent means ₹2.5 crore in your pocket.'

Connect rewards to real wins. Link top-ups or refreshers to milestones declaring 'Launch v2, and earn 0.1 per cent more'. That keeps equity fair and motivating.

And don't forget liquidity. ESOPs are promises of future value, but they must be perceived as real. Host a bi-annual ESOP Town Hall to explain dilution, review the pool, and, when possible, offer small buybacks for vested employees. It builds trust and shows that ownership here actually means something.

When you execute an ESOP with the same care you build your product, you unleash a powerful flywheel. And then your team doesn't just work for you, they bet on themselves through you. Your team no longer clocks hours; they chase the runway. Suddenly, every bug fix, sales closure, every milestone, and customer delight becomes a step towards mutual upside. That's incentive alignment at its finest, and it's the heart of a drama-free cap table.

Mindset Cue: When ESOPs are clear, fair, and tied to real milestones, they become more than compensation. They become commitment engines.

Co-founder Conflict and Equity Clarity

Nothing sinks a promising startup faster than a co-founder silently fostering a grudge. As shared in The Team Mindset chapter, co-founder harmony is non-negotiable. Yet nothing strains it more than unclear equity and ownership. You can fix bad code or a failed launch, but unspoken equity expectations quietly rot trust from within. And that's how equity ambiguity turns into resentment.

One founder feels they're pulling the entire cart. Another thinks they were 'promised' a bigger stake. A third silently questions, 'Wait, why do I still own the same percentage when I'm doing triple the work?' Here appears the need for a crucial mindset shift!

Founders often postpone equity conversations to maintain 'good vibes'. But often, a casual handshake deal today becomes a courtroom hearing tomorrow. When relationships sour, people remember the cap table more than the pitch deck.

> **Mindset Cue: Equity isn't a trophy for early participation. It's an unambiguous reflection of contribution, commitment and continuity.**

It's imperative for the co-founders to legalise and protect their shared vision against future contingencies. Unless you're okay with WhatsApp chats becoming your tribunal defence, it is non-negotiable to keep following clauses in your founder agreement on Day 0 itself. These 'must-have' clauses secure the team, not individuals.

- Reverse Vesting: Even for co-founders, equity should vest *after* the value is created, not before. Reverse vesting lets you reclaim unearned equity if the co-founder exits early.
- Decision–Deadlock Mechanism: What happens when there's a 50/50 split on a big call? Define a tie-breaker: bring in a trusted board of advisors and assign weighted votes based on role relevance, not on personal biases.
- Exit Triggers: Life happens. One founder wants to leave, gets poached, or just burns out. Define what counts as a good leaver versus a bad goer. Set rules for buyback pricing, IP ownership and transition timelines.

In co-founder relationships, the worst scenario strikes when one of the founders wants to quit suddenly with least objectivity. This hits the bigger challenge: planning a noiseless exit. It's unlike any employee leaving. This is the fork in the road where friendships get tested, and lawyers quietly lean in. But it doesn't have to turn into a courtroom drama.

Handled with maturity, a founder exit can reinforce trust both inside the company and among external stakeholders.

When a founder decides to step away, don't let it become a battleground of emotion and ego. Start by opening the books. Bring in an independent third-party valuation to anchor the discussion in data. Let numbers shape the deal, not memories. If the 'exiting' founder has made meaningful contributions, consider activating good leaver terms.

Partial vesting is not charity; it's recognition. It sends a message of fairness and protects team morale. And remember, an operational exit doesn't have to mean a full disconnect. Offering an advisory role or consulting arrangement can preserve institutional memory, reassure investors, and keep the relationship intact. How you handle an exit often sets the tone for future trust or future troubles.

Mindset Cue: How you handle exits often signals more about your startup culture than how you handle growth.

Atlassian demonstrates a classic example of co-founders who had complete clarity around ownership from the very beginning.[3] When Mike Cannon-Brookes and Scott Farquhar co-founded Atlassian, they didn't take outside capital for years.[4] But from Day 1, they had a clear founder agreement braced with explicit vesting terms, voting mechanisms, IP ownership, everything. They split the equity 50:50, but included reverse vesting and deadlock resolution clauses, even though they were best friends from university. Their logic? 'We might be mates today, but business has to survive our moods.'

Their alignment let them focus on building, not bickering. Fast forward. Atlassian today stands at a staggering valuation of over $42B, and both founders still co-lead the company. No dilution drama. No ego wars. Just product, process and people. 'We didn't need to fight over who gets how much. We each knew what we were bringing to the table,' said Mike Cannon-Brookes.

> **Mindset Cue: Set structure while the vibes are good. Friendship doesn't protect the business. Clarity does.**

In stark contrast, BharatPe stands out as a cautionary tale.[5] The company gained fame in 2018 with its UPI QR code innovation, attracting hundreds of millions in funding from top VCs. But by 2022, co-founder Ashneer Grover had been suspended amid disputes over governance and equity.[6] With no clear exit clauses, voting rights, or deadlock rules, a small disagreement turned into a public boardroom battle. The result: frozen ESOPs, demotivated teams and a tarnished brand momentum.

Unclear equity rules not only slow growth, but they can also blow up your team. Nail down your clauses before you need them.

The Mindset Shift

Beyond Excel maths, equity is a vehicle for trust, alignment and accountability in motion. It determines how founders stay united, how teams stay motivated, and how investors stay confident. When shared with clarity, it fuels momentum. When handled casually, it breeds confusion and cracks culture.

Smart founders treat the cap table as a living agreement, not a legal formality. They trade equity for value and employ dilution as a lever to grow, not as a means to avoid losses. They design ESOPs that feel fair and real, turning employees into believers and mutual beneficiaries.

Mastering the Equity Mindset means respecting the principle of ownership with fairness, transparency and shared value, eventually building legacies that outlive term sheets. Ultimately, it's about how ownership is earned, shared and honoured.

10

The Story Mindset

Pitching Without Pretending

Your startup isn't a one-act play aimed at a single crowd. It's a grand production with multiple audiences. *Investors* sizing up your vision for scale. *Customers* wondering if this solves a real pain. *Employees and partners* craving purpose, possibility, alignment and credibility. Each group brings its own hopes, fears and questions. And as a founder, your role is to build a single core narrative and tune its tone, detail and emphasis so that everyone sees themselves in it and leans in to become part of it. That's the Story Mindset – the skill of crafting every pitch, demo and conversation into an authentic, resonant story that draws in everyone, without resorting to hype.

In this chapter, you'll learn how to craft a unifying vision that resonates personally with each stakeholder, no matter their role or background. You'll discover how to tailor your language to bridge the gap between technical minds and emotionally driven believers, ensuring both feel aligned. Through the power of storytelling, you'll learn to inspire, recruit and fundraise, often all at once. And most importantly, you'll gain the tools to test, refine and adapt your narrative on the go, so your message always stays fresh, relevant and compelling.

Mindset Cue: Startups don't storify products. They storify possibilities.

Most founders obsess over what they're building – things like dashboards, features, backend systems, integrations etc. That's natural. But the truth is, be it an investor, a customer or an early employee, no one joins you just for what you're building. *They join you for what it could become.*

Your startup isn't a product. It's a promise of a better, faster, simpler solution, which has potential to unlock growth for all. And that promise, when articulated well, becomes the fuel behind every pitch, hire, sale and partnership.

Let me explain it this way. I once saw a founder demo a logistics tool to a room of bored faces. Until one pilot customer shared how the platform helped his team discover a broken distribution route that was losing them ₹30 lakhs per quarter. Suddenly, the room sat up. It wasn't the tech that won attention. It was the outcome. The possibility.

A product says: 'Here's what we've built.' A possibility says: 'Here's what it does for you.'

Why does possibility win over product? Because people may rationalise with logic, but they decide with emotion. When Airbnb started, it wasn't selling a rental platform. It was selling the idea that anyone could feel at home anywhere, and that emotional pitch resonated far deeper than any feature list could. Simon Sinek popularly quotes, 'People don't buy what you do; they buy why you do it.'

MVPs evolve, pricing changes, road maps pivot. But whether it's a founder fixing a pain they lived with, or a user whose life was transformed, a powerful narrative gets retold, remembered, and shared across tables, timelines and term sheets.

Would you rather hear 'We're building an AI-based health monitoring app' or 'Imagine never having to second-guess your heart health because your watch warns you before anything feels wrong'? Which one sounds more compelling? What sounds like a possible solution? The former sounds flat, while the latter drives a convincing narrative. Founders often think they need to 'pitch like pros' when in reality, they need to connect like humans.

That simple shift. The bridge from what you're building to what it can do, explained in simple words, is where real storytelling begins. It makes your startup feel inevitable. Desirable. Necessary.

What Makes a Founder Story Work?

Let's be honest. Most early-stage founder stories sound like this: 'We saw a huge market opportunity... built a scalable platform... targeting Gen Zs with an AI-powered solution... blah blah disrupt blah.' It's boring, generic and forgettable.

A powerful founder story doesn't start with a TAM slide. It starts with *you* and the clarity of thought behind *why you*, *why now*, and *why this*. This '3-why framework' blends Simon Sinek's and Andy Raskin's strategic narrative approach.

Let's break it down.

'Why you' reveals your origins. No one's asking for your résumé. They're asking for your reason. What is the itch that keeps you up at night? Investors and early teammates want to know your personal stake.

When Shashank Kumar and Harsh Songra started DeHaat, they didn't spin stories about 'agritech transformation'. They grew up in farming communities. They knew how broken the supply chains were and how smallholder farmers got the worst deals. Their story wasn't MBA-derived. It was root-level real.

If you've lived the problem or served those who have, say it. That's your edge. That's what makes you credible when things get messy (and they will). People don't back tourists in a market. They back locals.

'Why now' captures your timing tailwind. Good stories have urgency. Is there a market shift, a tech enabler, or a timing advantage that makes this the right moment to build it? Why does this problem feel ripe for solving today, not five years ago or later?

When Aadit Palicha and Kaivalya Vohra launched Zepto, grocery delivery wasn't new. BigBasket and Grofers were already around.[1] But India's post-pandemic consumer had changed. Instant-gratification culture had gone mainstream, and logistics APIs had matured enough to make 10-minute delivery possible. Their 'why now' wasn't convenience; it was the collision of behaviour shift and infrastructure readiness. Timing made 'quick commerce' believable and fundable.

Founders who nail the 'why now' don't look like dreamers. They look like surfers who spotted the swell early and started paddling before everyone else.

'Why this' exhibits your approach. Let's say your background checks out, and your timing makes sense. The next step is to ascertain that out of all the ways you could solve this problem, why this particular approach?

Let's take a comparatively new venture, Sleepy Owl. The founders weren't the first to sell coffee. However, they observed that Indian urban millennials loved coffee but hated the brewing process. Their 'cold brew in a bottle' wasn't a tech innovation. It was a positioning and convenience insight. They simplified a ritual, and that made it work.

This part of your story is about showing thoughtfulness. Maybe you're not building a 10x larger product, but a 10x simpler one. Maybe you're starting small, but with a deeply underserved niche. The point is your approach reveals your thinking.

The best founder stories don't have fancy punchlines; instead, they have clarity, conviction and a little unfinished business. Answer these '3 whys' right, and even if you're early, people won't care that you're not polished.

Avoid the Startup Theatre

There's a fine line between storytelling and showmanship. And too many founders cross it without even realising it. Here comes the startup theatre – decks packed with buzzwords, slides fluffed with jargons and grand claims that even founders themselves don't believe. The result? Hype kills credibility faster than silence.

Most founders fall into this trap because they feel pressure to 'sound big' to win cheques, and accelerators' ten-slide templates only reinforce that urge. Worse, mimicking the same over-polished format feels safer than trusting your version.

The moment you overstate traction, shouting '10,000 users!' when you only have a handful of engaged pilots, your audience's trust begins to evaporate. Don't pretend to be bigger, faster, or more 'game-changing' than you are. Think back to that demo where half the room was checking phones instead of your slides. Chances are, your product pomposity didn't interest your listeners. Early believers, such as investors, partners and hires, are smart. They can smell hype from a mile away. So don't pretend.

How do you fix it? Sidestepping the theatrics, founders must go in plain English. If your dad can't grasp it easily, you've overcooked the jargon. Swap 'blockchain-enabled omni-channel SaaS' for something tangible and human, pointing 'what real problem does it solve today?' Show real traction, however modest. Saying 'ten pilot customers loved your product and collectively saved ₹2 lakh last quarter' speaks far louder than a vague promise of 'on track for 100K ARR'.

Take the early days of Calendly.[2] Founder Tope Awotona didn't dazzle investors with bloated feature slides or market-size fireworks.[3] He told the story of his own pain – the maddening back-and-forth of scheduling meetings. Instead of a feature list, he described the relief of just sending a single link and having people pick a slot. That clarity, that honesty, helped him cut through the noise. It wasn't a performance. It was truth wrapped in simplicity.

Admitting 'we're in beta, but three out of five users call us indispensable' shows you listen, learn and iterate. Every stakeholder values these traits. So don't worry about being polished. Embrace imperfections. Authenticity is magnetic. Worry about being believable. Admit you're still iterating. Celebrate real user feedback, even the awkward ones. Trimming the theatrical fat not only sharpens your pitch but also invites your listeners to lean in, join the conversation, and believe in the real story you're telling.

The Three Stories Every Founder Must Master

Most first-time founders believe they need one story – *the investor pitch*. Well, will you narrate your investor pitch to your first customers and expect it to work its magic? In truth, in today's heterogeneous startup ecosystem, a single story rarely persuades everyone. Each stakeholder has a distinct psychological trigger and a different lens through which they evaluate a startup's potential in light of their interests. What excites investors might not impress customers or inspire early hires. Investors look for momentum and money. Customers look for relief from their pain. Early hires look for purpose and mission.

So, instead of a one-size-fits-all narrative, founders need three stories that play distinct roles and serve different objectives for different audiences. One ignites your mission. Another makes your product unforgettable. And yet another one earns you credibility in a room full of sceptics.

Each story, every narrative activates a different mental model.

- *The Vision Story* satisfies the emotional need for purpose.
- *The Product Story* answers the cognitive need for clarity.
- *The Fundraising Story* triggers the need for analytical confidence in transactions.

Try swapping one for another, and you'll see friction. Tell a VC your emotional origin story without metrics? You risk sounding naive. Explain ARR growth to a potential hire without explaining why it matters. You'll sound hollow. Like tools in a Swiss Army knife, each story has its distinct utility and mastery lies in knowing when to deploy which.

Let's unpack each narrative arc to unveil how storytelling becomes strategic rocket fuel.

The Vision Story

This is your 'why we started' heartbeat. This narrative is primarily shared with early believers, crucial hires, PR, podcasters, journalists, or that random guy you meet at a conference who asks the 'why' behind your startup. It cultivates identity and emotional resonance.

Narrate the problem that kept you tossing in bed at 2 a.m., someone's struggle you couldn't ignore, or a personal brush with the pain you vowed to heal. Something like 'I watched local artisans fighting to reach buyers, so I built a platform that brings global demand to their doorsteps.'

When Razorpay's founders spoke of the awkward calls to bankers explaining failed transactions, they weren't reciting figures. They were inviting listeners to experience the spark that lit their mission. Your origin story gives your startup a soul that sticks with people long after your deck has been minimised on the screen. It leverages your innate signalling to early believers that this mission is larger than a business plan.

The emotional trigger starts with your own friction point – the moment you couldn't unsee the problem. Link that moment to a larger mission, one that turns others into believers.

The Product Story

This brings you to zoom in on the problem-solution dance: 'What we do?' This is the tale you tell during demos to prospective clients, in customer discovery calls, and in onboarding sessions for new hires. If the origin story is your emotional hook, the product story is the clear line from pain to promise. It answers, how exactly do we get from 'Ouch!' to 'Ahhh'. Skip the laundry list of features and lean into a simple scenario: what did life look like before your product, and how does it feel now? It must hit a psychological trigger assuring instant relief and clarity about what you do using some simple scenarios. It's like 'Your team spends ten hours a week on client reports. Our tool turns that into three clicks and five seconds of reporting.'

Take Slack as an example.[4] Early on, Stewart Butterfield avoided selling it as 'corporate chat software'. He highlighted the real pain – teams drowning in emails, fragmented threads, and missing context. Instead of pushing features, he allowed prospects to experience a preview that showed conversations converging into a single searchable, real-time stream. The objective was clear: drive teams to 2,000 messages, because once they crossed that point, 93 per cent stayed – having felt the shift from friction to flow.

The Fundraising Story

This story is obviously aimed at your investors, the angels, HNIs, VCs, banks, or strategic partners, where building credibility, showcasing potential, and sparking urgency become target outcomes of the story.

Mindset Cue: The three-sentence rule works best for powerful product stories. Take your audience through the before, the breakthrough, and the new normal.

You walk into the pitch room excited to explain your customer journey funnel, your product's v2.0 launch calendar, and the seven integrations you've planned for next quarter. But your investor, though nodding politely, is quietly wondering, 'Is this the right jockey? Is the race even worth betting on? And why does this founder look so sleep-deprived at 11 a.m.?'

Investors aren't product users. They're probability hunters. They're scanning for asymmetric upside that can actually survive. When you ask for money, you're not seeking kindness. You're inviting a calculated bet. Your story must clear the investors' 'fundability filter'. Not with fancy tech, but by showing three things: you see what others miss, you can make it happen, and momentum is already on your side.

Mindset Cue: Investor brains are not wired like yours. Founders see a road map. Investors hear a riddle.

Look at OYO Rooms in its heyday.[5] Ritesh Agarwal didn't lead with 'we have X rooms'.[6] He told the story of ₹50 bookings and 85 per cent occupancy in Tier-2 cities, then painted a picture of a pan-India network unlocking ₹100 crore in GMV within months. That blend of micro-traction and macro-vision triggered a FOMO cascade among investors.

So lead with your strongest, smallest win. Then bridge to the horizon with concrete milestones and timelines. Something like: 'We've proven our model in three metros. Now with ₹3 crore, we'll expand to ten cities and unlock ₹30 crore ARR by Q4 2026.'

Think of your pitch less like a TED Talk and more like a movie trailer. Introduce the hero (you), the villain (the unsolved pain), and the breakthrough (your startup). Leave them curious, not crammed.

If you want the cheque, pitch the change, not just the chart.

Mastering the Chameleon Shift

Great founders don't just tell one tale. They forge the mindset with a smart manoeuvre – the Chameleon Shift. They know exactly which narrative to deploy, and when to amplify data, emotion, or vision. This narrative agility allows them to pivot from origin to product to fundraising, turns casual listeners into convinced ones.

In real-world scenarios, belief isn't built in a single pitch. Rather, as a founder, you might have to weave two or more story flavours with an intelligent choice of the right details in the right tone to the right audience at the right time.

Testing and Sharpening Time

You can't think your way into a great story. You talk your way into one. Pitching is not a writing exercise. It's an audience sport. You test it. Break it. Rebuild it. Then test it again.

Startup storytelling is more of a stand-up comedy. Comedians don't assume a joke is funny. They try it on an unsuspecting crowd and let the groans, giggles, or glassy stares decide. Smart founders do the same with their pitch.

If you're still tweaking bullet points in isolation and calling it 'refinement', you're missing the point. Your pitch isn't ready when you finish writing it. It's ready when strangers start leaning in, not just nodding politely.

Mindset Cue: People don't buy tickets for your pitching event again and again. Chances to impress diminish after a flop show. Thus, be a miser on takes.

Test like a comic, not a copywriter. Test your pitch in places where people can actually hear you, and be honest about it. Think over a steaming cappuccino at your neighbourhood co-working cafe, or in the chaos of a college hackathon. Even those awkward elevator rides with other founders or that ruthless, critical sibling who can smell fluff from a mile away. These are your trial stages. The format doesn't matter. What matters is whether your words land. It doesn't need polish. It needs to punch through the noise and be felt.

How do you know if your story is working? Simple. People start responding before you're done talking. Maybe they interrupt with, 'Wait, say that again?' Maybe they accurately paraphrase your idea five minutes later. Or they ask, 'Where can I try this out?' These are green lights. But if their eyes glaze over and they check their phone midway through your second sentence, it's a timeout for you.

A compelling story isn't a lecture. It's a spark. It should stir curiosity, raise eyebrows, or prompt a smirk. If it provokes no response, it requires work.

Drop terms like 'AI-powered optimisation infrastructure' unless your audience is made of robots or the room is packed with techies. Instead, say, 'It helps you pick your top three tasks without spending three hours making a list.'

Mindset Cue: Clarity beats cleverness. Simplicity scales.

Figma's early pitch is learning. Figma didn't start with a heavy product deck. Their core line was simple: 'Design together, in the browser'. At a time when design meant bulky software and endless file versions, this sounded almost too simple. Radical? Yes. Clear? Absolutely.

Memorable enough to win over designers – and eventually investors? Without a doubt.

Whether at meetups, dorms, or startup mixers, that pitch was tested in the wild, and it worked not because it sounded big, but because it sounded real.

Your startup story is a living prototype. Like an MVP, it's never final. You keep iterating. From casual coffee chats to sceptical friends, pitch it to 50 people and watch what connects and what falls flat. Notice which parts bring clarity and which fade into confusion. Then refine, rewrite and retell until your story feels effortless and truly resonates.

The best founders don't wait for perfection. They build stories that evolve with feedback, friction, and just enough public failure to make them unforgettable.

The Mindset Shift

The most compelling startup stories are the most believable ones. Those that instantly make people nod and think, 'Of course this should exist for sure.' That's the moment you're chasing when the fog lifts, the logic clicks, and the value feels obvious. It's not about drama or flash. It's about a story that feels so clear and inevitable, it earns instant trust. What makes your story stick isn't the adjectives. It's the alignment when vision, voice and value click in one breath. That mix of clarity, conviction and curiosity turns strangers into believers and even sceptics into listeners. That's what makes a story stick.

As a founder, you're not just selling a product, a feature or a deck. You're inviting people to believe in a vision that feels certain to happen and to become part of it. That's the power of storytelling done right. It makes your startup sound less like a bet and more like unmissable destiny.

11

The Capital Mindset

Fundraising with Clarity and Control

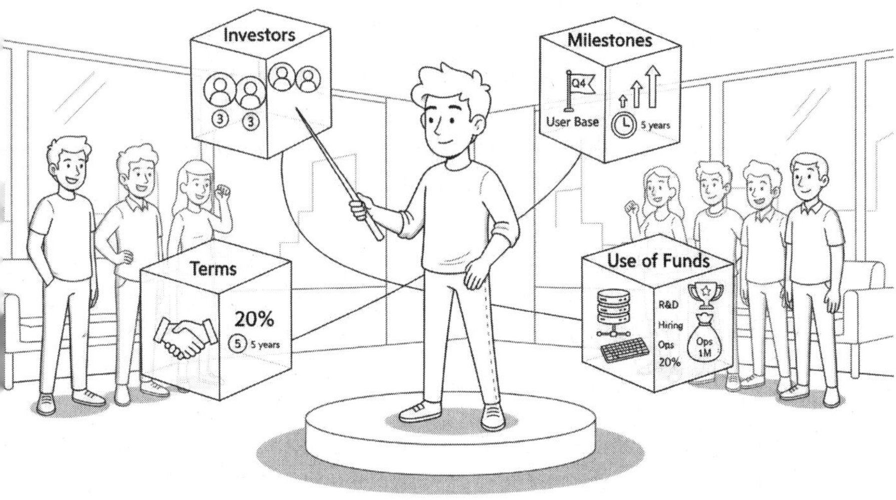

RAISING MONEY DOESN'T MAKE you a successful founder. It makes you a funded one, and there's a world of difference. Fundraising is a high-stakes decision with long-term consequences on your vision, your velocity, and your very role as a founder. It isn't a milestone; it's a multiplier. The moment you raise capital, you stop building for your shifting excitements and start building under watch.

Investors don't just fund your product; they buy into your decisions, your discipline, and your trajectory.

Fundraising indeed is a power move. But only if you play it right.

As Stripe's founder Patrick Collison puts it, 'Great founders treat fundraising as a means to an end, not the end itself.' That mindset alone separates the visionary builders from the distracted fund-chasers who dwell in the intoxicating pool of valuation and rounds-business.

Yet in the startup world, raising funds is often treated as the main event. The media loves screaming valuation numbers, and founders often end up celebrating their fundraising round louder than the actual product they're building. And somehow, a cheque in the bank starts feeling like a trophy on the shelf.

Well, it's not. Fundraising is neither a shortcut to building right nor a guarantee of fast growth. It won't fix a broken model or compensate for poor execution. What it does is amplify both your velocity and your vulnerability. Get it right, and you unlock acceleration. Get it wrong, and you lose control of the very thing you set out to build.

In this chapter, we're going to demystify the fundraising jungle. No fluffy buzzwords. No VC-worship. Just raw, real insights on when to raise, whom to raise from, and how to do it like a founder who's building something worth betting on. We'll cover the timing, the players, the story, the fine print, and most importantly, the mindset that brings out the disciplined capital allocator in you. Whether you're eyeing your first angel round or prepping for a term-sheet showdown, this chapter will equip you with the clarity, courage and control to treat capital not as a crutch but as a catalyst.

The 'When' and 'Why' Behind It

Most founders raise capital either in panic or in vanity. Panic, when the bank account starts looking like a desert. Vanity, when they see peers announcing rounds on LinkedIn and start feeling left out. Neither ends well.

Fundraising should never be a knee-jerk reaction. It should be a calculated, strategic decision anchored in your startup's actual momentum, not in FOMO or fantasy. Knowing when to raise is half the game. And it starts with tuning in to your own signals, not someone else's noise.

Here's a hard truth: investors aren't funding your Instagram followers, app downloads, or the PR buzz. They're looking for evidence that *something is working* – and can keep working under pressure. They look for real traction signals, not vanity metrics.

Factual traction is about showing that users are returning, not because you're dangling discounts – but because they genuinely want your product. That the conversion rates are improving, which means your messaging, funnel, or experience is compounding. And that the unit economics are holding strong as you grow, instead of falling apart with scale.

Take TinyOwl and Zomato. Both players dived in the food-tech race of the 2010s.

TinyOwl raised aggressively, expanded rapidly and focused on flashy app installs and discount-driven order volumes.[1] But its growth was artificially inflated, and was built on promotions rather than product stickiness. User retention dropped once the offers dried up, and the logistics strained under scale.[2] Despite raising over $27 million, it collapsed under its own weight.

Zomato, on the other hand, played the long game.[3] With menus, reviews and discovery, it started with content, building organic traffic and SEO dominance. It monetised later, layered services carefully, and scaled logistics only when core engagement metrics made sense. By the time it raised larger rounds, it had built a loyal user base, strong brand equity, and predictable usage patterns. Zomato raised $4.59 billion across 25 funding rounds.[4] Investors weren't just betting on growth; they were backing something hard to beat.

TinyOwl and Zomato were chasing the same opportunity. TinyOwl sprinted on discounts and speed, while Zomato took the slower path of building brand, community and habits. The difference showed up in the outcome.

Daily active users (DAUs) might look like an attractive metric in a pitch deck, but unless it translates into stickiness and revenue, it's just digital vanity. Investors seek predictability over peaks. They want to see signals that your business is not just moving, but moving in the *right* direction and on its own legs.

Ask yourself, 'If I stopped all marketing spend today, would my core engine still run?' If the answer is no, you may not be ready to raise. You may just be dressing up noise as narrative.

Mindset Cue: Money buys you time, but only if you're watching the clock. Your burn rate is how fast you're spending cash. Your runway is the amount of time you can survive at that pace.

Think of fundraising as a clock that's always ticking. If you have nine to twelve months of runway, you're in a good spot. That's the time to prepare, to refine your pitch, to get your numbers in order, and to start building warm relationships with investors. At six months, the clock gets louder. That's when you begin real conversations, calmly and clearly, not in panic mode. But if you're down to three months or less, you're sitting on a ticking bomb. Options shrink. Leverage vanishes. Unless your traction is extraordinary, you'll be negotiating under pressure and deals made under stress rarely end well.

Observe the case of Housing.com.[5] They spent blindly upwards on celebrity ads, billboards and partnership tie-ups, even as its core listings engine and customer conversion process were still unproven. By the time it had six months of runway left, user engagement was flatlining, and the product hadn't found a stable revenue path. Desperate to keep the lights on, they raised a down-round on harsh terms, surrendered board seats and underwent a painful leadership reshuffle. All because their runway vanished before they'd validated their model.

Now compare that with NoBroker. They tested for two years with almost no spending. Growth came from word-of-mouth and referral loops. Once they hit 20 per cent monthly growth and demonstrated that landlords would pay, they raised seed capital in 2016. With clear metrics in hand, the valuation spiked 3x higher than peers. A full year of runway secured. Only then did they scale marketing. It compounded traction, not burned it.

Capital should not be a last-breath strategy. The best time to raise is when you've already found momentum and want to amplify it, not just to extend survival.

Your round should buy you time to hit the next real milestone. Maybe that's hitting $1 million ARR or achieving product–market fit, or proving retention in a new segment. If your goal is just 'to survive another 12 months', you're probably not ready to raise. Rather, you're trying to buy time for something you haven't yet validated.

Avoid the 'Too Early' and 'Too Late' Traps

Great founders don't raise because they're desperate. They raise because they know what the money will unlock. Too early? You give up too much equity for too little capital. Too late? You don't own the cards.

Raising too early often means giving away equity before you truly understand your company's potential. It's like pricing a product before you've even seen how customers use it. Founders who raise too early always find themselves over-diluted, under pressure, and locked into premature promises. This is called the dilution trap.

Take Clubhouse. They raised about $112 million in early funding at a unicorn valuation, before proving real product–market fit and broad user engagement. Hype and capital pushed expectations sky-high, but users didn't stick at the levels investors hoped once the novelty eased. Rather than fuelling sustainable growth, the money ended up magnifying the gap between expectations and reality. The money didn't fuel growth. It magnified the miscalculation.

On the flip side, raising too late means you're out of options. And that's when bad deals, lost leverage, and dictated terms find you. You're forced to accept punishing terms, offer steep discounts, or scramble for bridge rounds at awful valuations that only delay the eventual fall. You are late, and your runway is running short! So, you don't have the upper hand. That's what a desperation deal looks like!

In 2017, Stayzilla was growing but running on thin fuel. It delayed raising follow-on capital while competing with giants like OYO and Airbnb. By the time it reached investors, the runway was nearly gone. Debts were mounting. Leverage had vanished. The shutdown came soon after.

The smart move is to raise when you have proof – revenue, retention, engagement. Enough to show the engine works. But not so late that cash scarcity forces bad deals. That's when you hold the cards. You negotiate from strength and when you still have the upper hand, not from a place of panic.

Before you reach out to investors, run the *3C Rule*. First, *clarity*. Know the milestone you're raising to achieve. Second, *conviction*. Be clear about the evidence that will convince investors that your growth is real. Third, *contingency*. Have a backup plan if the round doesn't close. If you can answer all three, you're not just chasing capital. You're fundraising with clarity and control.

Who Brings What to the Table

Now that you've nailed the 'when' of fundraising, it's time to tackle the 'who'. Not all money is equal. Every investor brings more than cash to the table. Some add fuel. Some add friction. The key is knowing which cheque to accept and which to decline.

Money isn't a generic fuel. Every cheque carries the weight of expectations, clauses, and sometimes surprises. Before you sign, know exactly who's behind it and why they're writing it.

Early on, friends and family bring *emotional capital.* They back you, not your spreadsheet. Perfect for a small family-run pilot, but risky if you can't afford to lose both money and relationships. They support you at the earliest stage, often pre-product, when you just need trusted believers to get off the ground.

Once you have a working beta, some users, or early revenue, angel investors step in with *experience capital.* The right angel opens doors, shares scarred wisdom, and shortens your learning curve. The wrong one floods your inbox with forwards, meddles in your cap table, and drags you into endless weekend 'strategy' calls.

When you've shown clear traction with users, pilots and small revenues, you may need *seed capital.* This is the stage to hire key people, build features, and push towards a repeatable growth engine. Seed funds love vision plus velocity. But not all seeds sprout the same way. Some investors act like partners. They connect you to mentors, customers, and future backers. Others behave like valuation vending machines. They demand unicorn-sized promises on day-one traction.

Mindset Cue: Seed investors also set your first valuation anchor. Pick ones whose values and term sheets fit your own.

Once you've cracked a product–market fit and crossed strong metrics, say $10 million ARR or equivalent traction, you step into *growth capital*. This is Series A/B territory. Here, growth trumps storytelling. Data replaces dreams. Dilution starts to sting. VCs usually step in at this stage. They expect board meetings that feel more like hearings than hangouts. They track dashboards for every KPI like churn, cohorts, burn etc. They push governance and structure. If your legal, financial, or operational house is messy, don't invite them yet.

By mid-to-late stage like Series B and beyond, you may seek *strategy or scale capital*. Strategic investors and corporate VCs step in here. They bring distribution muscle, brand legitimacy, and access to new markets. They can open doors to acquisitions, partnerships and diversification. But beware, their intent shapes their value. Some move like glaciers. Some invest simply to peek at your playbook.

Mindset Cue: Always ask whether they are here to co-build or to watch. Intent matters at every stage.

The Fundraising Arc

Now that you know who to call and when, it's time to sharpen what you say. Fundraising is 30 per cent numbers and 70 per cent story, but not the bedtime kind. You need a narrative that hooks, convinces and proves. We already discussed this in the previous chapter, 'The Story Mindset'.

It's not just about *what* you pitch – it's *how, when*, and *to whom* you pitch. The biggest mistake founders make is recycling the same story across every round. That's like wearing the same outfit to every occasion. It may pass once, but soon it feels lazy, stale, and out of place.

Each stage demands a fresh mindset, a narrative, a message. What wins angels sounds naive to a Series A partner. What excites a VC sounds overstuffed to a corporate investor. The trick is to evolve your story without losing authenticity while remaining grounded in numbers.

At the angel stage, your pitch isn't about precision. It's about belief. The product may wobble, the revenue may be zero, but if you make someone think, 'This founder will figure it out, no matter what', you've done your job.

Take Kuku FM.[6] The audio platform raised early angel money on one sharp insight: India's next billion internet users won't speak English. Their narrative was simple but bold.[7] Vernacular content was the future. They paired that with early pilot data and founder–market fit rooted in regional understanding.

The angels didn't see ARR. They saw clarity. They saw a team obsessed with the right problem, for the right audience. At this point, your pitch is founder-first. A lean six to eight slides deck works. Hit the pain point. Show your obsession. Explain what a $5,00,000 cheque unlocks in terms of validation and learning.

Mindset Cue: It's not about dazzle. It's about conviction. Show grit. Show obsession. Show you're coachable.

Once your MVP is live and a few hundred or thousands of users are engaging, your story shifts gears. At seed, it's about validation and velocity. Investors aren't just betting on the team or the dream anymore. They're scanning traction, product insight and a real path to product–market fit.

Look at Dunzo. Before the big Google-backed rounds, it raised seed money with nothing more than WhatsApp screenshots. The product wasn't even an app. It was a chat-based concierge service. But it had repeat usage, sticky demand and a clear urban pain point. The story wasn't about scale. It was about habit.

By seed, your pitch must cut sharper. Show how early adopters behave. What they love. What they hate. How much does it cost to acquire them and retain them? Don't inflate. Share the learning curve. If your CAC is high, admit it. Then show the path to improvement.

This is also where a great go-to-market narrative helps. Who are you targeting next? Why now? What will a million dollars unlock that changes your velocity fundamentally?

Mindset Cue: You're not selling dreams anymore. You're selling proof. Show that your engine has started to run, even if it coughs once in a while.

As you crack product–market fit, you step into early Series rounds. Here, the game changes. Investors stop playing poker. They start reading your balance sheets like forensic auditors. You must prove the engine works. It's clearly predictable, repeatable and expandable now.

Take Teachmint.[8] The edtech infra platform raised $20 million in Series A funding on the back of rapid user growth and a teacher-first focus. But growth alone didn't clinch it. What won investors was clarity. They showed why CAC was low, why teachers stayed, and how each rupee spent unlocked outsized returns. Growth with levers, not luck.

By this stage, founders need to zoom out. Investors expect to see dashboards, CAC-to-LTV dynamics, burn ratios, revenue projections, risk matrices and governance structures. If you're vague, you're toast. No fluff. No ego. Just clean signals and brutal honesty.

Mindset Cue: You are now a capital-efficient operator. Think like a CFO. Speak like a board member. Pitch like a leader who has scaled, seen storms, and built systems for more.

As you move to late-stage rounds, the story shifts again. It's no longer about proving you can build a company. It's about showing that you can lead it to a strong outcome, an IPO, an expansion, or an exit while holding your ground.

Look at Lenskart. By its late rounds, it wasn't just about growth. It was about dominance. Brand equity, omnichannel presence, repeat customers, sharp unit economics – SoftBank wasn't buying a dream. They were buying defensibility, vertical integration and global ambition backed by structured leadership.

Late-stage decks aren't glam. They're loaded with budget forecasts, hiring maps, compliance dashboards, market-share defences and multiple exit paths. At this point, even strategic investors like corporate VCs or partners join to access your ecosystem. They can add muscle, but be aware that some move slowly and others complicate exits.

Mindset Cue: You're now in capital allocation mode. Your pitch should reassure, not excite. You're not painting visions anymore. You're presenting engineered outcomes.

In truth, your startup's journey is one long narrative. But your pitch generally evolves. Angels want belief. Seed wants proof. Series A wants mechanics. Late-stage wants predictability. Founders who adapt without losing authenticity stand apart.

So don't just tell your story. Tailor it. Stage by stage. Because your cap table depends on it.

Negotiating Terms

Let's say you've just closed a ₹5 crore round at a ₹40 crore valuation. Fancy tweets go out. LinkedIn celebrates. You pop the headlines. Media cheerleads. Now take a breath and read your term sheet again. Because here's the uncomfortable truth: *valuation grabs the spotlight, but terms control the steering wheel.*

And while you were dreaming of growth, somewhere buried in the fine print are clauses that could haunt your cap table, your autonomy and your future exit. This is where many founders go wrong. They optimise for vanity over sanity.

But terms aren't side notes. They're *the actual contract* – the term sheet. They decide who holds the power, who makes decisions, and who walks away with what when the music stops.

Let's decode these terms and technicalities, founder-style.

Liquidation Preference

In simple words, it is the term sheet that governs who gets paid first and how much when your startup liquidates, or is sold. Certainly, it's not always you! Here's how this works: say you raise ₹10 crore on a ₹40 crore post-money valuation. You think, 'Hey, I still own 75 per cent. If I sell the company for ₹50 crore tomorrow, I'll get most of that, right?'

Wrong.

If your investor has a 1x liquidation preference with a *non-participating clause*, they receive ₹10 crore off the top. You and the team split the remaining ₹40 crore. But if it's participating preferred, they take ₹10 crore *and* their equity share of the rest.

Now imagine a 2x liquidation preference with participating rights. That same ₹50 crore exit leaves you with morsels. It's not just about how big the pie is. *It's about who gets the first slice, and how many servings they're allowed.*

Pro Rata Rights

It's like a VIP pass for early investors. It gives existing investors the right (but not the obligation) to invest more money in future funding rounds in proportion to their current ownership. As a result, they don't get diluted. When new money pours in, these rights ensure old money doesn't get pushed to the sidelines. In short, it's investors saying, 'If you're raising again, don't forget to save me a seat at the table!'

Sounds harmless, right? Just a clause that lets your early investors double down in the next round.

But here's what happens: if Investor A puts ₹1 crore in your seed round at a ₹10 crore valuation, they own 10 per cent.

Later, you raise a ₹10 crore Series A at a ₹40 crore valuation. Without pro rata rights, Investor A can't invest again, and their stake drops to 7.5 per cent. However, with pro rata rights, they can invest ₹1 crore again to maintain their 10 per cent stake. In essence, pro rata rights let early investors keep their slice of the pie as the company grows, protecting them from dilution and rewarding their early faith.

Now, you're the one getting diluted further. The pie hasn't grown, but more people are demanding the same slice. Pro rata rights are not inherently problematic, but they matter only when your startup becomes hot. And by then, you're the one fighting for breathing space.

So be aware. Set ceilings. And negotiate scope. Because 'friendly angels' can become *very* protective of their slice when things take off.

Anti-Dilution

Anti-dilution suggests who bears the pain when valuations drop. This clause protects investors by adjusting their share price or ownership if the company raises future funding at a lower valuation than they originally invested, so they don't lose value when things go south.

Let's say you raise Series A at a ₹100 crore valuation, but your Series B ends up happening at ₹60 crore – the down round. Your investors may have anti-dilution protection, which means they receive additional shares to maintain their percentage without putting in more cash. That's called *weighted average protection*.

A nastier version of this clause is *full ratchet*. It's a type of anti-dilution protection where, if the company raises money later at a lower price per share, the earlier investor's original investment is converted as if they had invested at the new lower price.

In simple terms: if they bought shares at ₹100 and a new round happens at ₹50; their earlier shares are adjusted as if they too had paid ₹50. This effectively increases their shares without investing more. It's beneficial for investors, but tough on founders. As it causes heavy dilution for the founding team and other shareholders. You absorb all the dilution and lose shares and control.

This clause alone can wipe out early team equity and kill morale when it's needed most.

Valuation Versus Control

Getting a ₹40 crore valuation looks glorious in a tweet. But what if that cheque comes gift-wrapped with invisible handcuffs? You celebrate the round, but a few months in, you realise control shift. Now, you can't hire a senior leader without investor sign-off. You can't pivot the product without a board resolution. You can't say yes to an acquisition offer, even a life-changing one, unless your investors agree.

In short, you're still CEO, but now with a boardroom above your head, and a leash around your road map. This is what control loss looks like. This is what they call 'selling the steering wheel'. And it rarely shows up in pitch-day excitement. It manifests in difficult decisions, missed targets, and course corrections.

Mindset Cue: Great startups are built and evolved through iterations. If you need permission for every experiment, you're not running a startup. You're chairing a committee.

Let's break this down. High valuations often feel like a win, but they frequently come with strings. That big round may bring along investor veto rights over key decisions such as hiring, firing, fundraising or acquisitions. You might still hold majority equity on paper, but lose board control in practice. Add to that lock-in clauses that restrict your ability to exit, take a sabbatical, or even pivot unless the board signs off.

You may think, 'It's fine. These are supportive investors.' But power changes people. And priorities. Your ten-year vision might conflict with their five-year funding cycle. What feels like alignment today can turn into *active interference* tomorrow.

Instead of obsessing over the highest valuation possible, ask, 'What will this cap table and power dynamic look like two rounds from now, when I've raised ₹50 crore more, and I'm no longer the biggest shareholder?'

Because the goal is not just to raise money. It's to retain control long enough to build something meaningful. Ryan Breslow, the founder of Bolt, walked away from a mega valuation to preserve his team's independence. He stated that a high valuation with the wrong terms is like a beautiful mansion with no deed. You'll live there, but you won't own it.

So don't just negotiate for money. Negotiate for manoeuvrability. Don't sell the steering wheel.

Learn to spot the landmines. Here's a short list of founder nightmares dressed in legalities:

Clause	**Why It's a Problem**
Full Ratchet	*If your next round is at a lower valuation, you take all the dilution. Investors stay protected. You shrink.*
Founder Vesting Reset	*Makes you re-earn equity you already built. Demoralising and controlling, like starting from zero again.*
Board Control Grab	*More investor seats than founders? Three investors. Two founders. Suddenly, your board becomes a courtroom and you're the one being cross-examined.*
Veto Rights Overreach	*Need approval for every move – hiring, funding, product changes. Fast becomes frustrating.*
Overreaching Drag-Along	*They can force an exit, even if it's not the right time or price for you. Your company, their call.*

Don't fall for 'standard clause' talk. Ask. Challenge. And if you don't understand something, don't nod along. Delay, ask a lawyer, and decode every word before you sign.

Bhavish Aggarwal, the CEO of Ola said it in an interview, 'We almost lost control of the company before we knew what was happening. You think the term sheet is a formality. It's not. It's the game.'

Term sheets are not templates. They are negotiation leaves. Every clause can be discussed. Every term is a trade-off. And you, the founder, are not just raising money – you're defining the power dynamics of your company for years to come.

So, go beyond the headline number because the real deal isn't in the funding news. It's in the footnotes.

Due Diligence Drama

Due diligence means a full-blown audition, your moment in the hot seat. And no, it's not the part where the investor makes up their mind about *whether* to fund you. It's where they validate *why* they should trust you with their capital.

At this stage, you've likely impressed them with your pitch, your deck is tight, your numbers look promising, and your vision is inspiring. But now comes the real test. Can you prove you're not just a passionate founder, but also a disciplined driver of money, operations, equity and legal sanity?

What is *due diligence* really? Well, it's a cross-check, a trust test, and a risk-mapping exercise rolled into one. For investors, due diligence is how they protect their downside. They're not just writing a cheque of $2 million for you. They're entering a multi-year marriage.

They want to know mostly everything that matters. Is your financial data solid or stitched with assumptions? Are your legal and cap table structures clean and investible? Can you, as the founder, handle scrutiny, pressure and governance?

For founders, it's a mirror. It shows how ready your house is for guests. Are your books clean? Are your IPs and shares sorted? Are you mentally and structurally prepared to lead a company with investor oversight?

Messy spreadsheets? Missing founder agreements? Unclear ownership of your codebase? Unstable cap table? Bad accounting? Structural randomness? Questionable founders' credibility? Even one crack can delay or derail the deal or lead to painful renegotiations right when you're running out of runway. Everything you pitched and beyond is validated on the ground.

That's why you don't just need a checklist. You need a survival kit. Because due diligence done right doesn't just close rounds, it builds credibility for the rounds to come. So, before your investors hit the deep dive button, make sure your house isn't just clean. It's inspection-ready!

Here is how you do it.

The first and foremost consideration is *financial hygiene.* This is the first room investors walk into. And like a messy living room, it tells them a lot about founders' dealing with money.

Your profit and loss statements, burn rate, cash flow and expense trails must not look like abstract art. They should narrate a clear story: where your money comes from, where it goes, and how long it'll last.

Here's what serious investors want to see. First, clean books. No 'miscellaneous' black holes – every expense tagged and reconciled. Second, monthly burn reports. No guesstimates, rather, verifiable numbers. Show monthly cash burn side by side with your key milestones ('₹40 lakh burned ➔ +30 per cent month-on-month [MoM] users'). Third, revenue breakdowns – cohort-wise, product-wise, customer-wise, geography-wise, depending on your stage. Last, your unit economics: CAC, LTV, payback period, churn, retention curves. You definitely earn bonus points for dashboards that show these in motion over the past six to twelve months.

Mindset Cue: If your finances look like a puzzle, investors won't try to solve it. They'll just pass.

The second important consideration is *legal reconnaissance.* In this room investors peek into your statutory structure, authority, ownership, and binding agreements. Even a single poorly documented share allotment from two years ago can tank a deal.

Here, investors will dig deep into your paperwork before signing a cheque. They'll start with incorporation documents and filings with statutory body, checking if what you show in the deck matches what's filed on paper. No ghost shareholders should pop up later.

Next, founders' agreements. These must spell out vesting schedules, roles and exit clauses. Without them, you risk 'surprise resets' when things get tough.

Then comes IP ownership. If your tech co-founder is still freelancing elsewhere, that's a red flag. Investors want proof that your code, design, logo, patents and every other IP asset legally belong to the company.

Employee ESOP records are another hot spot. Have they been issued? Is the pool formally structured? A casual promise via email doesn't count.

And finally, cap table clarity. No invisible shareholders. No old SAFEs drifting around. No undisclosed convertible notes. What appears to be a 15 per cent dilution on a slide can balloon into 30 per cent when the documents surface.

Many startups stumble at this stage and lose the funding game before it even begins. For instance, GovWorks, a disruptive public-government bridging platform in the 2000s, had to delay its Series A by five months because a dormant co-founder still legally held 20 per cent with no vesting clause. Don't let old ghosts hold your startup hostage.

Further, the least discussed consideration, yet most crucial in due diligence, is *founder readiness*. It's the silent deal-maker, often underestimated but deeply scrutinised when it matters most. Due diligence interviews aren't just box-ticking exercises. They're designed to assess you as a founder: your clarity of thought, grasp over your numbers, and composure under pressure. Investors aren't just funding your startup. They're betting on your ability to navigate chaos with conviction. They read you, your maturity, clarity and judgement.

You are grilled on tough questions like:

- What's your backup plan if your top channel gets saturated?
- What would you do if you had to cut 40 per cent of your burn overnight?
- How do you decide between growth and profitability?

But how to get ready for such unexpected turning interviews? There are no comprehensive cheat sheets for this, right?

Well, the best advice is not to prepare answers. Rather, prepare *clarity*. Investors want to see how you think, not just what you say. Don't recite scripts – internalise your numbers and strategies so you answer with genuine confidence. *This isn't just a data room test – it's a founder fitness test.* Can you handle the stress, the ambiguity, and still operate like a responsible custodian of capital? That's the test!

Lastly, here's the curveball – the final consideration that most founders overlook. Due diligence eats time, and time burns money, and that's what the invisible cost of capital is. Time is the real burn.

A typical diligence cycle can take six to eight weeks, even longer if your documents aren't sorted. Meanwhile, your team needs leadership, your product needs you, and your burn doesn't pause. *That's why the smartest founders treat fundraising as a parallel operation, not a desperate manoeuvre.*

Factor a *'time tax'* into your runway: if diligence takes eight weeks, that's eight fewer weeks of product work. Start early or tighten operations to avoid scrambling. Also, maintain a lightweight data room from Day 1. Just a set of folders on the drive or cloud – finance, legal, team, product metrics. Keep it tidy. Updating it monthly or quarterly means you're never caught scrambling when diligence begins.

During due diligence, founders often encounter a quiet punch that they didn't prepare to combat – the *dilution double tap.* Raising capital and eventual dilution aren't just about valuation. It's about *how, where* and *when* dilution is applied. Something that can dramatically impact your ownership maths and your payout later.

Why is it called the dilution double tap? Well, because you get hit twice!

The first tap is when, on an investor's insistence, you create an ESOP (option pool) before the investor puts in money. That pool comes out of your equity, not theirs. And the second tap occurs when you give up more equity to the investor as the round closes.

Result? You're giving away shares for both future hires and for new money, while the investor's stake stays untouched. You lose twice; they don't.

Let's decode it with a simple example:

You're a solo founder holding 10,00,000 shares. Before your ₹5 crore seed round at a ₹20 crore pre-money valuation, your investor insists on creating a 10 per cent ESOP pool. Here goes the maths,

Pre-money valuation = ₹20 crore
Founder Initial Shares = 10,00,000
Initial Share price = ₹20 crore ÷ 10,00,000 = ₹200/share (Pre-money and pre-ESOP)

Now begins the actual shift dynamics as we discuss creating a 10 per cent ESOP or Options Pool.

Case 1: When the founder creates a 10 per cent ESOP pool before the investment/pre-money

When investors insist on a 'pre-money ESOP pool', what they really mean is: 'Let's carve out 10 per cent of the post-money fully diluted cap table – but do it before we pump in our ₹5 crore.' That way, the pool sits outside their 20 per cent stake, and you absorb the full hit.

Let X = ESOP shares.
Total pre-money shares = 10,00,000 + X.
Price per share = ₹20 crore ÷ (10,00,000 + X)
Investor shares = ₹5 crore ÷ price = 5 crore ÷ [₹20 crore ÷ (10,00,000 + X)] = 0.25 (10,00,000 + X)

After the round, investors want X = 10% of the new total (founder + ESOP + investor).

That Implies, X = 10% of [10,00,000 + X + (0.25 (10,00,000 + X))]

Solving this equation yields:

- X ≈ 1,42,857 ESOP shares
- Total pre-money shares = 11,42,857
- Price/share ≈ ₹20 crore ÷ 11,42,857 ≈ ₹175
- Investor shares ≈ ₹5 crore ÷ ₹175 ≈ 2,85,714
- Total post-money shares = 10,00,000 + 1,42,857 + 2,85,714 = 14,28,571

In this case, the post-money cap table appears like:

Stakeholder	**Shares**	**Ownership (%)**
Founder	*10,00,000*	*70*
Investor	*2,85,714*	*2*
ESOP (Pre)	*1,42,857*	*10*
Total	*14,28,571*	*100*

Case 2: When the founder creates a 10 per cent ESOP pool after the investment/post-money

here, we first add investor shares, then carve out 10 per cent for ESOP:

Price/share remains ₹200 (₹20 crore ÷ 10,00,000)
Investor shares = ₹5 crore ÷ ₹200 = 2,50,000
Post-investment pre-pool total shares = 10,00,000 + 2,50,000 = 12,50,000

ESOP = 10% of 12,50,000 = 1,25,000 shares
Total post-money shares = 13,75,000

In this case, the post-money cap table appears like:

Stakeholder	**Shares**	**Ownership (%)**
Founder	*10,00,000*	*72.7*
Investor	*2,50,000*	*18.2*
ESOP (Post)	*1,25,000*	*9.1*
Total	*13,75,000*	*100*

Here comes the contrast:

	Pre-Money ESOP (%)	**Post-Money ESOP (%)**
Founder Ownership	*70*	*72.7*
Investor Ownership	*20*	*18.2*
ESOP Ownership	*10*	*9.1*
Total Shares	*14,28,571*	*13,75,000*

Founders often overlook how ESOP pool timing impacts their ownership. If the pool is created after the investment, dilution is shared, and you might hold, say, 72.7 per cent instead of 70 per cent. But a pre-money ESOP setup dilutes you even before the cheque lands, pulling your stake down. It also dips your share price immediately – ₹200/share versus ₹175/share – because the new capital hasn't yet come in.

Investors often push for pre-money clauses, since it lets them buy a bigger slice. Maybe 20 per cent instead of 18 per cent. While the difference looks small on paper, across multiple rounds, that ownership delta can snowball into millions.

Thus, always anchor your negotiation with a clear share price. Check whether the ESOP pool is pre- or post-money. Negotiate the option pool post-money. Ask that the ESOP pool be created *after* the investment. In this way, dilution is shared with the investor. Quite a fair game.

In the end, nail diligence with sparkling books, airtight legal docs and rock-solid confidence. Then, model your cap table moves in advance – so you steer the deal, instead of watching it steer you.

Mindset Cue: Don't just celebrate a term sheet. Scrutinise what's behind the numbers. Ownership isn't just about how much you hold, but how much you control and how much you take home when the music stops.

Capital Deployment Discipline

You survived diligence. You charmed investors. You've raised the capital. The funds have landed. Congrats. Now what? This is where most founders stumble – not at the raise, but at the *spend*. Fundraising is not the finish line. It's the starting gun for a race you can now run faster, but only if you know where you're headed.

Don't burn it all in the first lap. Operating discipline isn't about spotlights, but it's survival. Just because your runway got longer doesn't mean you are licensed to run recklessly.

Take OYO's post-Series B story. Flush with capital, it expanded rapidly – thousands of rooms, dozens of countries. But the burn caught up fast.[9] What followed was a painful round of layoffs, restructuring and public scrutiny. Even Ritesh Agarwal admitted later: 'We had to learn cash discipline under fire.' Lesson? Don't spend like a unicorn; think like a bootstrap, and you try to capitalise every penny. Your capital must go towards two things: validating assumptions or scaling what's already proven and working. And always, budget for curves, bumps and breakdowns. Startups rarely follow straight roads.

Now that the money has arrived. You're being watched, not just by your team and users, but by your cap table, by your new stakeholders. 'Investors fund ambition, but they reward discipline,' says Reid Hoffman, the co-founder of LinkedIn. You change your mindset to focus on metrics instead of cheques. Flashy dashboards may win short-term praise, but they don't build long-term trust. What gets respected are metrics that show maturity. For instance, as you pace up with fresh fuel, you keep a very close eye on your survival metrics. You watch CAC trend as you optimise channels. You track MRR/ARR with surgical precision to ensure that your month-on-month growth is more heartbeat than hiccup. And you drill into cohort retention to assess whether users are staying, engaging and paying. Or are they ghosting? Because nothing kills momentum faster than those one-time users that never return.

Peter Drucker said it best: 'What gets measured, gets managed.' Thus, having a proper hold on your real meters keeps you above and ahead of the game. And in today's market, what gets managed gets funded.

Paytm cracked its early monetisation code by focusing on transaction frequency and ecosystem stickiness – not just downloads. That shift helped them convert casual users into power users, and gave investors a clearer view of monetisation potential.

Capital is like nitro. Handle it right, and you fly. Mishandle it, and you blow up. With fresh capital in the bank, confidence runs high. The road map looks exciting. Spend plans feel justified. But amid all that ambition, one force stands quietly between wisdom and waste: **your board**.

Think of the board not just as post-facto reviewers of your slides but as real-time brakes and balancers to your capital decisions. They aren't there to approve your shopping list. They're there to ask the hard, uncomfortable questions before that list turns into burn.

As soon as investors come on board, your board becomes a living pulse-check on your judgement. You're not just steering the business. Instead, you're explaining, justifying, and sometimes defending how you plan to turn money into results. Not with jargon. Not with hype. But with clarity and control. Yes, they can open doors and provide strategic guidance. But their most underrated role? Disciplining your capital allocation, decisions and directions.

Let's discuss Naveen Tiwari's InMobi. Their early board meetings weren't feel-good updates; they were sparring sessions surcharged with real talk about failed pilots, churn concerns and pricing chaos. Founders' honesty in board meetings helped them dodge costly mistakes and develop smarter strategies more quickly. Looking back, that honesty wasn't just helpful; it became their secret weapon.

So, the board isn't just there to monitor you. If used well, they discipline your decision-making, especially when the cheque has already cleared, and you think no one's watching. You'll know you're maturing as a founder when you stop pitching to your board and start co-problem-solving with them. Because a well-used board can protect you from your own optimism, and in startup life, that's half the battle.

The Mindset Shift

You've got the cheque now. Great. Now show what you can turn it into. Budget with intent. Track like a watchdog. Allocate for returns. Govern like a grown-up. Raising money is not the finish line. It's the starting gate with sharper turns and higher stakes. A big cheque doesn't build your product. A fancy VC logo won't fix a leaky funnel. And a ₹50 crore valuation? That's not love from the market. That's just expectation in disguise.

The best founders treat capital not as fuel for fireworks, but as oxygen for growth. They raise not because the runway is short, but because the road ahead is clear. They know every penny raised comes with a question: *what will you turn it into*? So don't just raise. Reflect. What do you need to prove? What will it cost you beyond equity? And when the next round comes, will this one have made you stronger?

Raising capital is more than a transaction; it's a partnership. With every rupee you accept, you're also adding voices to your boardroom, expectations to your cap table, and stakes to your vision. Raise smart, negotiate shrewdly, and deploy with discipline. And you'll turn every investment into a catalyst for exponential impact.

12

The Bootstrap Mindset

Building Without a Cheque

NOT EVERY FOUNDER TAKES the VC expressway. Some don't get invited. Others politely decline the ride and deliberately choose a different road – unpaved, unmarked and often uphill. No flashy boards. No warm intros. Just cash flow, boldness and a ridiculous amount of resilience. That's bootstrapping.

It's not a compromise. It's not a contingency plan that triggers when you fail to raise. It's a choice. It's a mindset!

A mindset that's not about smaller ambitions or shorter runways but smarter adaptation, tighter control, and unapologetic ownership. If raising capital is like adding rocket fuel, bootstrapping is pedalling your cycle up a mountain – sweaty, slow and deeply strengthening. It is not forced by imminent failure to raise funds; it's a strategic call, a rebellious choice made by the founder.

When you choose to run bootstrap, your burn rate challenges your bank balance. Monthly revenue is your only runway. No media coverage. No cap table drama. Just paying customers and decisions that sting hardest when they go wrong. But that's where it gets beautiful because everything you build is real. Every sale earned, every process tweaked, every rupee accounted for.

You become wired for value. You hate waste. You measure progress in real terms, such as retention, repeat purchases, profitability, etc. You defend your margins like territory. You build not because someone backed you, but because someone needed what you were building.

Mindset Cue: Bootstrapping doesn't teach you how to raise capital. It teaches you how to raise your revenue charts.

When the cheques don't come, you don't panic, you pivot. You adapt. You make ₹10 do the work of ₹100. You ship fast. You sell faster. And in the process, you build sharper instincts, stronger systems, and a business that doesn't beg to survive. It earns its right to scale.

Bootstrapping is indeed no cakewalk. It's gritty, risky and often lonely, with no fancy boardroom steering you, just your co-founders, a few trusted advisors, maybe, and your own conviction at the top. However, when strategised right, it works. Look at Zoho. They scaled globally, stayed profitable, and never touched VC cash. Or say Basecamp which turned away investors and doubled down on building what users genuinely needed. And Zerodha? Built brick by brick, with zero external funding and full-throttle control.[1]

This chapter is not about bashing fundraising or venture capital. That's not the point. We're here to understand what it really takes to build without it. Why bootstrap? Who should bootstrap? How do you stay sane doing it? And when (if ever) should you switch gears and raise?

So, let's dive into how to build without a safety net!

When and Why to Bootstrap?

Bootstrapping isn't a Plan B. Instead, it can be your fastest route to clarity. For many founders, it's a deliberate and powerful 'Plan A'. When you build on revenue instead of raises, every customer payment becomes proof that you're solving a real problem. You don't need a glossy pitch deck to chase investor validation. You need customers who open their wallets for the value you have built.

Raising capital isn't free. It costs you equity, precious time in pitch meetings, the mental energy of chasing term sheets, and often cedes decision-making power to outsiders. In contrast, bootstrapping gives you the flexibility to call your own shots. Your boardroom is the feedback loop from paying customers, not a pitch panel. You answer to real demand, not to the clock of a fund's lifecycle. You chase revenue, not round headlines.

Most founders treat fundraising as the starting gun, lazily fantasising 'Once I have the cheque, I can start'. Bootstrappers flip that script. They know that revenue is real validation. When Sridhar Vembu founded Zoho, he didn't wait for VC term sheets. He chased paying users. He reinvested every penny earned back into the product, not PR. The result? A global SaaS leader that never gave away control.

Bootstrapping is an amazing route, but it's not for every founder or every business model. It isn't for you if any of the following cases describes you or your business:

- If you're building a *capital-heavy product* such as EV batteries, robotics or pharmaceutical technology, bootstrapping is impractical. These sectors require serious upfront investment just to hit version one. There are high fixed costs, such as warehouses, physical inventory, manufacturing, etc. You may find it impossible to scale without external capital as you forge ahead.
- If you're in a winner-takes-all market like delivery apps or social networks, where speed to market decides the victor and moving slow could be suicidal. You'll be outrun before you've even set up.
- If you need personal financial stability now and can't delay your salary for the first 12 to 18 months, bootstrapping may push you to burnout.
- And if you're someone who gets easily shaken by uncertainty, slow traction, or market pressure, the rollercoaster of self-funded growth might drain you fast.

You can embrace bootstrapping if:

- You thrive on a revenue-first model. If your product can generate money from Day 1, for instance, SaaS subscriptions, consulting projects pay fees, or D2C moves units for direct sales. In such cases, bootstrapping becomes not only viable but strategic. Each payment isn't just income; it's validation that you're solving a genuine problem.
- You seek to validate before scaling. Bootstrappers insist on proving every feature, channel and hire before

unleashing significant capital. You only scale what works and that saves time, money and headaches. Rather, you can continue scaling thereafter if your economics favour expansion without an external raise.

- You value building control over speeding capital. If you're allergic to unnecessary dilution or you fiercely value the ability to pivot without board approval, bootstrapping keeps your cap table and your decisions clean. You retain the freedom to steer the company exactly where you want it to go.

As Nithin Kamath shared his approach towards building Zerodha in an interview: 'We never felt the pressure to scale beyond reason because we didn't raise. That freedom helped us think long-term.'[2]

His words capture the 'why' behind bootstrapping perfectly. When you don't need to chase the next round, you're free to chase sustainable growth instead. Sometimes the best 'round' you ever raise is the one you never had to take. For many founders, bootstrapping is a strategic path to building real clarity, real resilience and real value.

Building Without Burn: Operating Like a Bootstrapper

Bootstrapped startups live under a different kind of gravity. There's no safety net of fresh cash to catch you when you slip. So you learn to operate lean, and that lean isn't about being miserly. It's about being surgical.

You don't bulk-hire to fill seats or burn six-figure sums on splashy brand campaigns. Instead, you earn every rupee, stretch every resource, and squeeze outsized returns on each investment. This produces what I call a 'lean catalyst'. You spot what doesn't work fast, cut it lean, and double down only on what customers truly love.

Consider Paras Chopra of Wingify. He built the first version of Visual Website Optimizer alone, in his bedroom. No fancy office, no outsourced development shop. Just him, a laptop, and feedback from a handful of early users. When those users paid and stayed, Paras reinvested the profits back into the product. No VC dollars, no dilution – just proven features earning their keep. Today, VWO serves global brands and fuels its own growth entirely from customer-driven revenue.

Bootstrapping isn't about miserly pinching pennies. It's about being sharp, playing with your available money and resources. Do it this way:

- *Don't hire until it hurts.* Let the pain of being understaffed drive your decisions. When you finally onboard, every new team member must move a revenue needle or unlock capacity you genuinely need.
- *Automate what you can't delegate.* Manual processes are slow, resource-intensive and error-prone. If a task takes more than a few minutes or repeats monthly, it's better invest in automation. That might mean a simple Zapier workflow or a lightweight CRM, not an enterprise suite.
- *Test small, scale what clicks.* Think of tiny experiments and invest just enough on say, landing pages, micro-campaigns and concierge services before committing months of development time or hefty marketing budget. If the signal is strong, double the bet. If it's weak, scrap it and move on.
- *Budget as if cash could vanish tomorrow.* Because sometimes, it will. Plan every quarter against possible contingencies. Keep a buffer. Ideally, two to three months of runway. Even when cash flow looks solid.

This bootstrap discipline breeds twofold benefits.

First, it brings resilience. So when markets wobble, you're set up to pivot, not panic.

Second, it sharpens focus. You hone in on what truly matters: your core product, core customers and core growth levers.

Operating like a bootstrapper teaches you to build muscle before you burn. It forces you to ask at every turn, 'Is this purchase, hire or feature essential?' And that ruthless question, asked early and often, becomes your unfair advantage when you finally have the resources to scale.

Driving Growth Without the Gasoline: Bootstrap Scaling

Without VC money, can we grow and scale? The short answer is yes! But you have to do it masterfully. A founder's grit lies in this, yes, against the popular notion that growth needs fuel and fuel comes at a cost!

Bootstrapping runs largely on two self-reinforcing growth engines:

The first one is *profit flywheels*. Imagine a tiny snowball at the top of a hill, gathering speed as it rolls. In bootstrapping, every sale, upsell and retention win is snow being added to that ball, and you reinvest it instantly into the next push.

You manage your margins incrementally. For instance, for a subscription-based product with slightly ascending margins, you offer an add-on service or premium feature that costs almost nothing to deliver. This trivially yet comfortably commands a higher price from the user. Use that extra margin to fund your next feature.

Once you know how to drive for higher margins gradually, the pivotal deal is not to let your profits sit idle. Rather, invest strategically. Channel them straight back into product improvements, customer support, or targeted growth experiments.

Early on, Mailchimp introduced paid plans alongside free accounts.[3] Revenue from those plans funded product enhancements, such as email automation, improved analytics, etc, which, in turn, attracted more paid users. Profits cycled back into features, creating a flywheel that helped Mailchimp grow into a marketing powerhouse without a single VC rupee.

The second growth engine is *organic traction*.

Organic channels may take longer to build, but they compound without additional cash outlay. I identified three effective organic propellers that have worked visibly well for bootstrappers.

First, leverage word of mouth, the oldest growth hack in the business books, still the strongest. When you delight your first hundred users, pushing above and beyond, they naturally become your evangelists. They tweet about you. They drop your name in their WhatsApp groups. Why? Because your product didn't just earn some bucks, it earned credibility. Credibility that cannot be earned even after pushing millions in meta ads.

This isn't just free publicity. This is high-trust, high-conversion marketing, done for you by real users. It's how people discover new products they actually trust.

No matter how many millions you burn on paid ads, if your product doesn't spark a genuine sense of worth among users, people scroll past. But when someone hears, 'Hey, I've been using this, and it's amazing,' their ears catch the reco. Their curiosity spikes. Their intent gets real.

Mindset Cue: In a bootstrapped journey, user delight is your best-performing growth engine. Serve the few, and they'll bring the many.

Secondly, set robust search engine optimisation (SEO) foundations. Every business goes online in no time these days. But just being online isn't enough. You need to be discoverable. That's where search becomes a game-changer.

People Google everything. Problems, tools, gadgets, books, flights, comparisons, alternatives, how-to videos, the list is infinite. If your business shows up as their search result, you don't just get traffic, you earn trust before a sales call even happens. That's why setting up a strong SEO growth engine early on is a high-leverage move for any bootstrapped founder. No flashy budgets required. Just smart, consistent content. You start with deep, evergreen content like in-depth tutorials that solve real user pain points, case studies showing real outcomes, benchmark reports that position you as an authority, and so on.

These assets compound. Over time, they start ranking on Google, bringing in steady, qualified traffic without you spending a rupee on ads. SEO is your stealth growth gear. It doesn't scream like performance ads. But it sticks around, keeps working, and quietly fills your pipeline.

Lastly, reinforce community engagement. It's about building a sense of belonging rather than merely branding. People don't just buy products. They join tribes. By engaging with your audience through communities, you create a space where users feel seen, heard and valued. Host webinars that share real insights, not just sales pitches, show up in niche forums like Reddit, Discord or Indie Hackers, and spark real conversations.

Better yet, nurture a small private group of power users. Those early adopters who love what you're building. Involve them in decisions, listen to their feedback, and they'll become your loudest advocates. Community-led growth doesn't scale overnight, but it builds trust, loyalty and organic buzz, just the perfect fuel for bootstrapped momentum.

Zoho never splurged on ad campaigns. They invested in thorough product documentation, vibrant user forums and developer meetups, creating a self-sustaining ecosystem that attracted new clients year after year.

Mindset Cue: Bootstrapped growth is about building long-term value perception while pacing forward steadily.

As a founder running on your own pocket, your goal isn't just more customers. It's lasting, more valuable ones. Extend customer lifetime value (LTV) by upselling, cross-selling, and delighting users. Shrink your cash conversion cycle by invoicing promptly, offering prepaid plans, or using retainer models. When you hire, make it count. Every new team member should either accelerate revenue flywheels or amplify organic reach. When you spend, spend only where it multiplies your existing gains.

In the bootstrap world, scale is a function of discipline. Choose sustainability over speed, and you'll build a growth engine that runs happily on your own steam.

Hard Choices, Real Freedom

Let's be honest. Bootstrapping isn't all roses. It is not for the thin-skinned. It's building a business with your own hands. No investor airbags, no safety nets, and definitely no fast lane. You move slower, bear the full weight, and feel every jolt on the journey.

But here's the twist. For the right kind of founder, the control, clarity and independence are worth every bruise. Let's get brutally honest about what you're giving up, and what you stand to gain.

When you decide to build on your own, the first thing you give up is speed. There's no room for vanity hires, flashy ads, or a 50-member sales team in one quarter. Growth happens, but it's steady. Built brick by brick, not rocket by rocket. There's no fundraising buzz or media spotlight. Your wins are quiet until they're not. Recognition comes from users, not investors. You focus on solving today's pain, not chasing futuristic dreams.

So why bootstrap? For control. Every equity point stays with you. No tense boardroom debates, no investor pressure to pivot or burn faster. You decide the pace. You stay loyal to your customer, not your pitch deck. Every rupee you earn comes from real users, not from someone betting on a spreadsheet. That's what creates tighter feedback, faster learning and deeper trust.

Perhaps the most underrated benefit of bootstrapping is that you unlock long-term clarity. Without the noise of funding rounds or artificial deadlines, you think in decades, not quarters. You don't sprint for metrics. You build for meaning.

Bootstrapping is the real test of a founder's emotional stamina. When your revenue plateaus, you can't afford your own salary, and you see your competitors raising millions, tempting away your team. It's only your personal grit that keeps you sane. The bootstrap path is lonely, and doubt whispers at every step. But the payoff in control, peace of mind, and ownership is unmatched. It's priceless for many!

Basecamp could've taken VC money.[4] They didn't. Founders Jason Fried and David Heinemeier Hansson chose profit over pressure. They built a simple project management tool, charged for it from Day 1, and focused on serving small businesses. They were not chasing unicorn status. Over the years, they remained intentionally small, profitable and proudly boring. Their user base grew steadily. They were clear – 'We're in it for the long haul, not the headlines.'[5] Staying bootstrapped gave them the freedom to build a business aligned with their values, rather than defaulting to Silicon Valley's expectations.

Bootstrapping isn't a leaner version of the VC game. It's a different game altogether. One where you trade speed for sovereignty, hype for depth, and outside pressure for inner conviction. It's not easy. But for founders who value freedom over fame, it might just be the most rewarding path there is.

Bootstrapped to Funded: Knowing When to Flip

Some founders choose to bootstrap forever and win. Others start lean, then flip the switch to raise capital on their own terms. Both routes are valid. *What matters is knowing which route fits your stage, your ambition and your business model.*

If you're building a sustainable, profitable, slow-burning business, and you're content with controlled growth and ownership, staying bootstrapped might be your best bet. It gives you full freedom, cleaner operations and no external pressure. But if your market is heating up, your product is working, and capital can help you scale faster than competitors, raising funds strategically can become a smart next step, not for survival but for acceleration.

Starting lean doesn't mean staying lean forever. For several founders, bootstrapping is simply a launchpad, not a life sentence. And some of the most compelling funding stories out there began after the product had already proven itself. The real founders don't raise to survive or experiment in the dark. They raise to amplify.

Mindset Cue: The golden rule? Raise from strength, not from struggle. Raise when you're ready, not when you're desperate.

Investors are far more excited about accelerating something that's working than rescuing something that's stalling. Bootstrapping gives you leverage because you've proven that you can build, ship and sell without a financial safety net. Such discipline signals the founder's true maturity.

Capital, when timed right, multiplies momentum. But when taken too early or too late, it becomes a liability.

Now the million-dollar question is, how does a bootstrapper identify when it's the time to flip to investor funds? Well, here's the sweet spot. Do it if all the following check boxes are ticked for you:

- You've proven the product works in the real world.
- Customers are paying, churn is low, and word-of-mouth is building.
- You can predict where growth will come from, if fuel is added.
- You want capital to scale what works, not to experiment unquestioningly.

The trick is timing. Again, to reinforce the idea, you rise from a position of strength, not as a cry for help.

For nearly eight years, Calendly's founder, Tope Awotona, poured every cent of Calendly's revenue back into the product. No investors, no term sheets, just relentless focus on solving real scheduling headaches. He waited until the solution resonated so strongly that millions of users made it part of their daily workflow, and the company was reliably profitable. Only then, in early 2021, did he raise a transformative $350 million round at a $3 billion valuation, not to stay afloat but to turbocharge expansion. That capital powered a major enterprise sales push, unlocked cutting-edge AI scheduling features, and opened doors in Europe and Asia. Today, Calendly is the go-to tool for more than 80 per cent of Fortune 500 enterprises, demonstrating that a founder who builds with conviction can invite investors on their own terms and turn smart funding into rocket fuel.

The Mindset Shift

Bootstrapping isn't the enemy of funding. It's just a different first chapter. If you play it right, it becomes your biggest strength in the chapters that follow. Because no one respects money more than the founder who's built without it. When you build this way, two things happen – you gain unshakeable conviction in your vision, and you develop the operational discipline that venture-backed companies often envy.

You learn to sell, to survive, to ship. VCs may fund you. But bootstrapping? It builds a radical mindset. And if you ever choose to raise, you do it not out of dire necessity but from a position of unmistakable strength, as you'll have already proven that you can build, adapt and thrive without a safety net.

Arc 3
Growth, Grit and Goodbye

13

The Traction and Growth Mindset

Validate and Multiply What Works

YOU HAVE RESOURCES NOW. Maybe investors trusted your vision. Maybe your customers paid their way into your journey. Either way, the question isn't just about having money or momentum. The real question is, *where do you put it?* Every penny, every hour, every bit of energy counts. Without knowing what actually works, it's easy to waste them chasing illusions.

Traction is your first proof. A small group of loyal customers. A feature people can't get enough of. A cohort that sticks around past the honeymoon phase. These wins aren't guarantees. They are signals that indicate your product, market approach, or execution is hitting the right note.

Growth is the next step. It's not about doing more for the sake of it. It's about amplifying what already works – doubling down systematically and building a repeatable engine. Many founders get stuck here. They celebrate early wins but fail to ask the crucial questions: *which signals are repeatable? Which are scalable? Where should I invest – time, money, talent – to get real impact?*

This chapter helps founders learn to spot real signals, rigorously validate them, and design growth systems that multiply success. You'll see how small wins become big proof – and how that proof becomes the foundation for real, sustainable growth.

By the end, you won't just know what traction looks like. You'll know how to turn it into leverage. So every action, every penny, every decision moves your venture forward.

Finding Your Signal in the Noise

Early signs of traction are usually subtle. A handful of customers are returning. There's a small spike in engagement. People are sharing their first-hand experiences and suggestions. Most founders miss these subtle signals because they're looking for fireworks – viral growth, huge revenue jumps and overnight success. That's noise. The signal is what actually tells you something is working.

The challenge is separating *real traction from vanity metrics.* Not every click, download, or page view matters. Some numbers look impressive, but don't translate into meaningful growth. Real traction shows repeatable behaviour, stickiness, and a willingness from your customers to engage consistently.

Imagine a new edtech startup launching a coding course for teens. The website gets 10,000 visits in the first month. Impressive, right? But only 50 students actually complete the free trial. Most founders would celebrate 10,000 visits. But the true signal is the *completion rate* – these 50 students are engaged, learning, and likely to pay for more courses. That's traction. Everything else is noise.

Once you identify these signals, the next step is understanding 'why they exist'. What product piece, messaging, or timing drove these behaviours? Observing patterns in small groups of early users can reveal insights that extend well beyond the initial cohort.

So, founders, you got to cut the noise out and derive real traction signals. Look into meaningful customer behaviour. Track engagement that shows commitment, not just curiosity. Check for early repeatability and product advocacy. Small, reliable signals are far more valuable than flashy, superficial metrics. They tell you what's worth multiplying.

Small Wins, Big Proof

Every startup's growth story begins with small wins. These wins may look minor on a spreadsheet, but they are proof points – validations that your product works in the real world.

The danger for many founders is dismissing these wins as 'too small to matter' or rushing to scale without understanding *why* they worked. The smarter approach is to treat small wins as prototypes for bigger strategies. What worked for ten customers can be refined and repeated for a hundred, then a thousand.

Meesho's early traction didn't come from fancy marketplaces. Their small win was enabling just a few homemakers and small resellers to sell through WhatsApp groups. That feature solved a clear problem – easy product distribution for non-tech-savvy sellers. The model clicked, and what started as small reselling networks became a platform serving millions of entrepreneurs.

The lesson is simple. Don't underestimate the power of small, repeatable wins. They are not just signs of progress; they are the foundation for scalable systems. Each win is evidence, a signal of traction, and when multiplied with focus and intention, the same signals become the backbone of sustainable growth.

Metrics That Matter

Once you've spotted the signals, the next step is tracking the right metrics. Not every number tells a story. Some are vanity; others are proof. Knowing the difference is crucial. Let me share three tested approaches to help you easily uncover your real traction.

First, founders need to focus on actionable metrics, not vanity ones. Page views, downloads and social media likes may look impressive, but they rarely indicate whether the business is truly moving forward. Actionable metrics, by contrast, measure behaviours that drive growth, retention and revenue. The retention rate reveals whether users keep coming back. The conversion rate shows how many visitors actually turn into paying customers. Cohort analysis uncovers whether early users behave the same way as later ones. These numbers don't just create a feel-good story – they reveal the real health of the business.

In the early days of Trello, millions signed up quickly, but downloads alone weren't the proof of value.[1] What mattered was how consistently teams kept creating and completing boards. By tracking engagement within boards – cards moved, tasks completed, projects shared – Trello spotted what drove retention. They refined the product around those behaviours, ensuring users stayed active long after sign-up. That focus on usage, not vanity metrics, powered Trello's global adoption.

Second, tailor metrics to your venture type. Metrics aren't one-size-fits-all, and what matters for a SaaS company is very different from what drives a D2C brand or an edtech startup. For instance, for SaaS businesses, churn rate, MRR, and active usage are core metrics which reveal both retention and engagement. While in the D2C or e-commerce space, repeat purchase rate, average order value, and CAC are critical for understanding customer behaviour and profitability.

Each set of metrics tells a different story, but in every case, the goal is to track what truly drives growth and validates your product-market fit. Take BYJU'S. Their early traction wasn't just about app downloads. They measured course completion rates and quiz engagement, which showed which lessons kept students hooked. That enabled them to optimise content and learning outcomes to scale the model successfully.

Lastly, combine qualitative and quantitative insights. Numbers tell you *what* is happening; conversations and feedback tell you *why*. Talk to your users, run interviews, and integrate the insights with your analytics. The intersection of data and real user behaviour is where true insights live.

Focus relentlessly on metrics that demonstrate real traction and predict growth. Track what indicates commitment and engagement, not just casual attention. These metrics become your compass for growth.

Customer Feedback Loops

Feedback is the clearest voice and verdict of your customers. Without a structured approach to gathering, analysing and acting on customer feedback, early traction can plateau, and small wins remain isolated sparks rather than engines of growth.

A feedback loop is more than just listening. It's a continuous cycle of observation, learning and iteration. Customers provide signals – sometimes subtle, sometimes loud – that reveal whether your product or service truly solves their problem. The goal is to turn these signals into decisions and improvements that multiply impact.

For instance, in its early days Intuit faced a critical problem with the usability of its flagship product QuickBooks: small business owners were confused by accounting jargon and complex workflows. Instead of relying only on internal assumptions, the team went into the field. They visited customers, watched them use the software, and listened to where they struggled.

These insights led to simpler language, cleaner navigation, and redesigned tasks that matched how owners worked. The result? Higher adoption and strong word-of-mouth growth. The feedback loop didn't just fix usability; it became a catalyst for scalable expansion. What Intuit did with QuickBooks represents what's sometimes called 'authentic learning through user immersion' or 'field validation'.

A strong feedback loop starts with steady capture – surveys, prompts, emails or interviews. Then, zoom out. You don't chase individual complaints; you hunt for patterns. Once you see the signal, act fast. Ship changes, test, measure. And always close the loop. You tell your customers that their input helped shape the product. It builds trust and keeps the feedback flowing.

Feedback loops are not optional; they are growth multipliers. Every insight, when acted upon, turns small wins into scalable outcomes. Treat your early adopters as co-creators of your product – they reveal the pathways from proof to leverage, from traction to growth.

Growth Mindset: From Proof to Multiplication

Traction is your proof. It tells you something is working. But proof alone doesn't build a company. The next leap is learning how to multiply it.

This is where the growth mindset kicks in. If traction is about discovering what works, growth is about designing systems that replicate, amplify and scale it without hiccups or breakdowns. The fuel may come from investors or customers, but fuel without direction burns out fast. The founder's challenge is knowing exactly where to channel energy, money and talent to create exponential impact.

Too many startups stall at this stage. They celebrate early signals, but then chase every glittery new opportunity instead of focusing on the few things that truly work. Growth doesn't come from doing more; it comes from doing more of the right things, in the right way, at the right time. Growth demands discipline. It's certainly not about pouring money into ads or doubling headcount overnight. It doesn't happen by chance. It is not accidental. It's the result of repeated experiments, careful measurement and deliberate decisions. Here is how it is engineered:

1. *Growth is multiplying, not just adding.* Many founders confuse growth with addition. More features. More marketing channels. More hires. But true growth is about multiplying what's already working, not scattering efforts everywhere.

   Razorpay didn't begin by trying to become a full-stack financial services giant. It didn't launch with lending, payroll, banking, subscriptions or neo-bank features. It focused on one painful problem Indian startups faced – making online payments easy to accept. At a time when payment gateway integrations were slow, documentation was messy, and onboarding was bureaucratic, Razorpay obsessed over developer-friendly APIs, faster activation and clean documentation. Instead of building everything at once, it removed friction. It simplified integration. It supported founders personally. And by multiplying that single strength – seamless payment acceptance – it became the default gateway for thousands of startups. Only after dominating that core did it expand into lending, banking and payroll.

> **Mindset Cue: Don't spread thin. Find the one lever delivering results and focus your energy on amplifying it.**

2. *Find your North Star.* Growth gets messy when teams chase too many metrics. DAUs, revenue, churn, CAC, retention – all matter, but not equally. Scaling companies rally around one North Star metric – a measure that reflects the core value delivered to users. It aligns teams and filters distractions, and when every department optimises for the same outcome, growth compounds in the right direction.

Say for Spotify, it wasn't downloads – it was listening hours. They optimised for time spent, repeat sessions and habit formation. Because in streaming, attention is the real asset. More hours. Stronger habit. Bigger moat.

> **Mindset Cue: Without a North Star, you chase vanity. With it, you build momentum.**

3. *Growth thrives on structured experiments.* It isn't about random hacks or lucky breaks – it's about running disciplined tests that reveal what truly drives traction forward. The cycle is simple yet powerful: test, measure, learn, repeat. Every experiment is built to answer one core question: if we change this variable, does traction increase in a meaningful way?

The process starts with a clear *hypothesis*. For example, you may believe that reducing checkout steps will improve conversion. Next comes the *experiment* itself – running a controlled test on a subset of users without disrupting the entire system. Then, *measure* the outcomes with well-defined metrics that leave no room for ambiguity. Finally, make the call: if the change works, scale it across; if it doesn't, discard it without hesitation.

This rhythm of disciplined experimentation is what transforms growth from a gamble into a repeatable system.

It helps founders move from gut-feel decisions to data-backed choices, while still leaving room for creative leaps.

Take LinkedIn for instance. They used constant A/B testing in its early years to refine user engagement. Features like 'People You May Know' came directly from growth experiments. It started as a small test, but once it proved effective, it became one of their strongest drivers of engagement and network effects.

4. *Turn experiments into playbooks, and playbooks into growth engines.* One test can spark a win. But lasting momentum comes from turning that win into a repeatable system. Capture what worked and why. Build playbooks for the big levers: onboarding, retention, referrals. That way, lessons don't vanish with memory or team churn, and execution is consistent, not improvised. Keep running fresh experiments. Feed the results back into the system. Each cycle makes the engine sharper. Growth then stops being about chance. It becomes discipline – learning, adapting, scaling.

Mindset Cue: Growth is less about guessing and more about running dozens of small, data-backed experiments.

HubSpot built its growth engine by systematising inbound marketing.[2] Instead of random campaigns, it created a repeatable funnel or a flywheel: blogs to lead magnets to free tools to paid subscriptions. Each step was measured, optimised and documented.[3] Over time, this engine became their unfair advantage, fuelling consistent growth without relying on unpredictable tactics.

5. *Avoid growth traps.* Not every spike is real growth – many are just illusions. Founders often fall into predictable traps. One is over-optimising acquisition,

Mindset Cue: Growth isn't a one-off trick. It's a system you build, refine and scale.

pouring money into ads while ignoring churn. Another is premature scaling, where teams hire aggressively, expand into new markets, or launch too many features before validating the core. A third is chasing virality – designing gimmicks that create a short-term buzz but fail to build lasting retention. These traps feel like progress in the moment, but they weaken the foundation and make true growth harder to sustain.

For instance, Hopin, a London-based virtual event and conferencing platform grew at lightning speed during the pandemic. It raised over $1.1 billion and reached a valuation of nearly $8 billion in less than two years. With physical events shut down during Covid, virtual conferences exploded in demand. Hopin expanded fast – acquiring companies, hiring hundreds of employees across dozens of countries, and serving thousands of organisations.

But the growth was driven by circumstances, not long-term behaviour. When in-person events returned, demand dropped quickly. The company had to lay off a large portion of its team. Hopin scaled for a moment in time, not for lasting habits.

Mindset Cue: Growth without validation is a collapse waiting to happen. Always check if the foundation is strong before multiplying.

6. *Build teams with growth DNA*. Growth isn't just about numbers or experiments. It's a culture. Companies that scale sustainably know this: growth cannot live in a silo. It's not something the marketing team handles while product, engineering or support sit apart. True growth happens when every function works towards the same North Star. That's why the best companies build cross-functional growth teams. These teams blend product managers who shape

features, marketers who understand demand, engineers who build for scale, and data scientists who track what works. Together, they ensure growth is part of every decision – from the way a button is designed and how onboarding flows, to how retention loops are built.

Take Facebook. They invented the playbook. They didn't leave growth to marketers only. They played cross-functional. Engineers worked on signup flows, designers tested onboarding tweaks, and data scientists tracked cohorts. By treating growth as a product problem – not a marketing campaign – they scaled from millions to billions.

Still, for many startups, growth remains a marketing KRA. They spend on ads, run campaigns and chase spikes – while ignoring friction, broken onboarding or high churn. The result is predictable. Money burns, but traction doesn't stick.

Founder as Growth Leader

Mindset Cue: Growth is everyone's job. When growth becomes culture, experiments turn into systems, systems into playbooks, and playbooks into scale.

Growth culture always starts at the top. In the early stages, your energy signals priority. By engaging in experiments, questioning assumptions, and driving learning loops, you show the team that growth isn't an afterthought – it's survival. The founder's energy makes growth contagious. Thus the founder stands as the company's default chief growth officer. And that remains a founder's non-transferable role. Founders often think growth can be delegated once a marketing head joins. That's a myth. In every company that scaled, growth was primarily a founder's obsession.

If founders treat growth as 'the marketing team's job', they create distance. But when they obsess over funnels, review retention data, sit in on customer calls, and challenge activation rates, they set the tone for the entire company. Growth isn't just marketing metrics. It's how well the product resonates. How fast feedback turns into fixes. How tightly the team rallies around a North Star metric. And nothing sets that tone louder than the founder's own actions.

Take Patrick and John Collison at Stripe. Payments were messy. Developers hated integration. So the brothers visited customers, sat with them, and installed Stripe themselves. This 'Collison' installation programme became legendary. It wasn't just support. It was a founder-led growth hack that made Stripe spread like wildfire.

Similarly, Byju Raveendran of BYJU'S used his teaching charisma as the first growth engine.[4] Byju himself conducted mathematics classes in stadiums to introduce thousands and millions of students to a whole new approach to learning, emphasising curiosity and conceptual understanding. He won trust. Those stadium sessions became the foundation of a billion-dollar edtech brand.

The pattern is clear. When founders chase growth themselves, momentum follows. Teams copy what founders care about. If a founder obsesses over growth, the culture absorbs it. If a founder ignores it, no one else treats it as urgent.

The Mindset Shift

Traction is the first whisper that your idea works. Growth is turning that whisper into a roar. One without the other is incomplete; traction alone stalls, growth without traction collapses.

Founders often forget that traction is not about vanity spikes, and growth is not about endless hacks. Both are about proving and then compounding what truly works.

So the founder's job is simple. Identify what works. Note small wins. And turn tested pilots into repeatable systems. Do that, and traction stops being fragile. Growth stops being luck. Together, they become momentum – the kind that compounds into scale. Traction shows it works. Growth turns what works into momentum. And culture ensures that momentum is sustained.

14

The Adaptive Mindset

Pivoting and Deciding with Clarity

TRACTION GIVES YOU CONFIDENCE. Growth gives you momentum. But markets have a way of humbling even the best founders. Customer behaviour shifts. Competitors respond. Capital dries up. Technology moves faster than your road map. Suddenly, what worked yesterday no longer works today. These are all signals of change.

This is where *adaptability* becomes a founder's most needed muscle. The hardest decision is not starting up. It is deciding whether to stay the course or change it. Every founder reaches a crossroads. Some things click, but others stall. The market moves, shifts, and changes the rules. At that moment, the founder faces the toughest call: *persist* or *pivot*.

The Adaptive Mindset is not about guessing. It is about clarity: of when to persist, when to shift, and how to separate actionable signals from distracting noises. Many startups fail not because they lacked effort, but because they held on too long to something that had ceased to work. Others die because they pivoted too often, never giving one path a fair chance.

Often, a pivot is misapplied as a dramatic overhaul. To do it right, a founder needs discipline, not panic. Decisions made in desperation only deepen the mess. Sometimes, changing the course can be as subtle as repositioning your product, or narrowing down to the customers who care the most, or adjusting your pricing. At other times, it's as big as rewriting your business model. The essence remains the same: a pivot is a strategic decision to realign with reality, a decision made on evidence and conviction. Evidence from data, customer behaviour and traction signals. Conviction rooted in the vision of why the startup exists in the first place.

This chapter unpacks how, as a founder, you can leverage resilience with an Adaptive Mindset, listen to the market, choose between gut, data and conviction, learn from legendary pivots, and know when staying the course makes the most sense.

Spotting Signals, Distilling Noise

The first step in determining whether to pivot or persist is to truly listen to the market. Many founders get this wrong. They mistake noise for signal. A handful of happy users, a spike in downloads, or even a glowing review can feel exciting. But those are just moments, not proof. What really matters are patterns.

Data, opinions and feedback surround every startup. Customers say what they like. Investors push what they want. Competitors reveal their moves. And the market itself keeps swinging. The hard part isn't hearing – it's knowing what deserves your attention.

Founders often fall into extremes. Some react to every single comment. Others ignore the signs until it's too late. Both are dangerous. One angry tweet doesn't mean you need a redesign. But if ten customers leave for the same reason, that's a clear signal.

Mindset Cue: The real skill is spotting repetition.

Listening to the market means watching consistent behaviour.[1] In 2009, Airbnb was barely surviving, making about $200 per week and close to running out of cash. While reviewing listings with Y Combinator's Paul Graham, co-founder Joe Gebbia noticed that all the New York photos looked awful, resembling cheap camera shots that made the rooms appear unattractive. They learned that guests weren't just looking for cheap stays – they wanted trust and unique experiences. On Graham's suggestion, the founders flew to New York, rented a camera, and personally took beautiful high-resolution photos of the hosts' spaces. That non-scalable, human-centred action doubled their revenue in a week and broke them out of their stagnation. It marked a mindset shift: they stopped trying to solve every problem with code and leaned into real-world empathy and experimentation. This core design-thinking insight changed Airbnb's trajectory.

Signals usually appear in three places. The first is *behavioural data*: do users return after the first try, or drop off? Do they invite friends, or keep it to themselves? Numbers show patterns, but only with context. The second is *customer conversations*. Honest feedback often hides in small moments – a hesitation during purchase, a blunt complaint, or a clever workaround. These reveal real needs. The third is *market shifts*. External changes can rewrite the rules overnight. Remote work fuelled SaaS adoption. Short videos reshaped how millions consume content. Startups that recognised these early gained an advantage.

Mindset Cue: Feedback will always be noisy. Data will always be messy. Markets will always change. But when you spot repeating behaviours, recurring complaints, or big external shifts – you've found a true signal.

The Adaptive Mindset begins here: learning to cut through the noise and act on what's real.

Pivot or Persist Dilemma

Every founder faces a brutal moment of truth: either stick with the original path or shift course. The choice isn't about ego. It's about survival.

Pivoting isn't failure. Persisting isn't stubbornness. The real challenge is knowing which one makes sense at the right time.

A *pivot* means you shift – sometimes slightly, sometimes drastically. It could be a new feature, a new market, or a complete change in how you deliver value.

Persist means you double down, betting that what you're building just needs more time, polish or reach.

When customers pull you forward – returning on their own, recommending your product, asking for more – you know you're on track. But when you're burning time and money only to keep them interested, it's not grit anymore, it's denial.

The market has its own language. If every push still leaves you stuck on a plateau, the market is telling you something. And sometimes, the world itself shifts under your feet – a new regulation, a new technology, a cultural turn. What was once a strength can turn irrelevant overnight.

Take Instagram's story of subtraction.[2] It didn't start as the sleek photo app we know. It began as Burbn, a cluttered check-in app. Users ignored most of its features, but one thing stood out – they loved sharing photos. That was the signal. The founders stripped everything else away and doubled down on photos. That pivot built a billion-dollar company.

On the flip side, look at Netflix in the 2000s. They had an option to pivot away from DVDs-by-mail when competitors loomed. But their data showed customers loved the service, and the market for DVDs was still strong. So they persisted. That persistence gave them time to prepare for their real pivot: streaming.

The Adaptive Cycle

Behind every smart pivot – or equally smart decision to persist – lies a repeatable cycle. Founders who've been through it multiple times describe it simply: **Observe → Test → Decide → Commit.**

It starts with *observation*. You tune into signals from users, markets and competitors. Not just vanity spikes or isolated praise, but patterns that reveal what's really happening. Are customers returning, or are they drifting away? Are acquisition costs rising faster than revenue? Markets don't lie, but they rarely speak loudly – you need to listen closely.

Next comes the *test*. Instead of betting the company on a hunch, you make a small, controlled move. Adjust pricing for one segment. Try a different distribution channel. Launch a stripped-down version of a feature. Small tests reduce the emotional and financial costs of being wrong, and generate evidence rather than opinions.

Then, you *decide*. Not based on hope or ego, but on results. Did the test improve retention? Did customers adopt the new feature willingly, or only after incentives? Data may not tell the whole story, but it forces honesty.

Finally, you *commit*. Half-pivots are confusing for the team, the customers and the market. Once clarity emerges, you move with conviction.

And then the cycle begins again. This loop never really ends. Startups live inside it. The faster and more honestly you run it, the better your odds.

The toughest stage in this loop is deciding the direction. At this juncture, founders typically rely on three forces: *gut, data* and *conviction*. Each can guide you. Each can also mislead you.

Gut instinct is fast. It is built on intuition, pattern recognition and past experiences. Many breakthrough decisions have come from gut calls. Steve Jobs trusted his gut when he killed the physical keyboard and insisted the iPhone should have a touchscreen. At that time, BlackBerry dominated, and data showed customers loved keyboards. Jobs believed people didn't know what they wanted until they saw it. His instinct told him the touchscreen was the future. He was right. But your gut can also trick you when you confuse personal bias for market truth. That's why relying only on instinct is risky.

Data offers evidence. It reduces the room for personal bias influencing your decisions. Numbers show what people are actually doing, not just what they claim or what you believe. But numbers rarely tell the full story. Raw numbers can mislead if you don't dig deeper. Early on, Duolingo observed high downloads but low retention. The team investigated, and the insight was sharp: learners felt lost without small wins. So they gamified progress – streaks, levels, rewards. Retention shot up, and Duolingo became the world's most used language app. The data showed a leak. The gentle pivot fixed it.

Conviction is the belief that the market has not yet matured, and going forward, the founder shall be betting on tomorrow's possibilities instead of today's realities. When Tesla was pushing electric cars, the data looked bleak. Adoption was negligible. Charging stations were rare. Analysts laughed at the idea of mass-market EVs. Yet Elon Musk's conviction in a cleaner, electric future kept the company moving through near-bankrupt phases. He persisted. Conviction gave Tesla time to survive until the numbers finally caught up.

The reality is – great founders rarely adhere to a single decision force. They blend them. Gut delivers speed. Data provides evidence. Conviction fuels persistence when both gut and data seem uncertain. Think of them as three lenses. Through one, you see chances. Through another, you see proof. Through the third, you see the prospects. The art lies in knowing when to switch lenses and when to trust the overlap between them.

Adaptive Mindset Played Right!

Adaptation looks modish in hindsight. But for the moment, it feels messy, uncertain and risky.

When Peyush Bansal started Lenskart, India's eyewear market wasn't a startup darling.[3] Most people still bought spectacles from the shop next door. Ordering glasses online sounded far-fetched. Lenskart stuck to eyewear as the core – the 'what'. But distribution was where they pivoted. They began online, soon realised trust was a barrier, and added home eye check-ups and trials. Later, they expanded into offline retail, blending online and offline long before 'omnichannel' became a buzzword.[4] The pivot wasn't in the product – it was in the channel. Persistence in mission, flexibility in approach. Today, Lenskart dominates India's eyewear market because it adapted.

Slack is another textbook example of a pivot. The company was originally building a game called Glitch. The game never scaled. It shut down. But the internal communication tool that the team had built for themselves? That became Slack. Rather than pushing harder for a failing game, the founders noticed a signal. People who tried their communication tool found it indispensable. They pivoted fully, turning a side utility into the main product. The result? Slack grew into one of the fastest-scaling workplace apps in history. What looked like failure in gaming became a billion-dollar success in team communication.

> **Mindset Cue: Sometimes the win hides in what feels like a side project.**

Zomato shows yet another form of adaptation.[5] It started as a simple restaurant discovery platform. You opened the app, browsed menus, and maybe called to book a table. Useful, but not transformative. The big shift came when they saw food delivery exploding globally. With the boom in smartphone adoption and low data costs in India, the timing was right. Zomato leaned into logistics, building one of the largest food delivery networks in the country. It wasn't an easy shift. Operations-heavy, capital-hungry, filled with risk. But it transformed Zomato from a discovery app into a daily-use product for millions.

The persistence? They stuck with food as their domain. The pivot? They shifted the value proposition from finding food to getting food. Today, that decision defines Zomato.

These pivots and persistence calls weren't random gambles. They were anchored in signals. Lenskart spotted trust gaps. Slack noticed what users loved. Zomato recognised market timing. Adaptation doesn't mean abandoning vision. It means adjusting the route while staying true to the destination.

When Adaptation Fails

Adaptation is not just about making changes. It is about making the *right change at the right time.* Some companies saw the signs but ignored them. Others made shifts too late or without conviction. Both mistakes proved fatal.

Spotting back in time, Kodak was not just *a* photography company – it was *the* photography company.[6] For most of the twentieth century, it dominated the global film business. Ironically, Kodak itself invented the first digital camera in 1975, when a young engineer built a prototype that could capture and display digital images.

But instead of leaning into this breakthrough, Kodak's leadership shelved the idea.[7] Why? Because they feared it would consume their lucrative film business. Their attachment to the present blinded them to the future. By the time Kodak finally tried to push digital cameras in the 2000s, companies like Canon, Sony, and eventually, smartphones had already won the market. Kodak filed for bankruptcy in 2012.

> **Mindset Cue: Founders must be watchful. Protecting their current model at all costs can sometimes cost them the future. A pivot delayed is often a pivot denied.**

Nokia shows how clinging to the old mindset kills giants.[8] In the mid-2000s, it was untouchable, owning 40 per cent of the global mobile phone market. Its devices were famous for their durability and reliability. Innovation wasn't missing either. Nokia had touchscreen prototypes and internet-ready phones in its labs long before Apple launched the iPhone.

The fall began when the world shifted. Consumers shifted from phones to smartphones, from calls to apps, and connected living. Nokia saw the signal but clung to Symbian instead of betting on a fresh platform. Even when Android emerged as an open ecosystem, they hesitated, convinced that Symbian could survive. By the time Nokia tied up with Microsoft, Apple and Android had built unshakable user and developer networks. The decline was brutal. In 2014, Nokia sold its handset business to Microsoft – a deal that itself flopped.

The story mirrors that of Kodak. Both had talent. Both had resources. Both glimpsed the future early. What they lacked was conviction. They froze when bold action was most needed. In fast markets, hesitation is as lethal as inaction. Slack and Zomato leaned into weak signals and struck gold. Nokia and Kodak second-guessed until it was too late.

The Power of Micro Decisions

Not every shift is a headline pivot. Sometimes it's the small, subtle decisions by the founders that decide whether a startup survives or fades.

YouTube wasn't born as the giant online video platform it is today. In fact, it started as a dating site where people could upload short clips about themselves. Hardly anyone did. The founders then made a minor adjustment: they opened the platform to *any* video. No grand press release, no billion-dollar strategy. Just a simple call: let people share whatever they want. That micro decision unlocked an avalanche. From viral clips to music videos, YouTube quickly became the internet's stage.

Pivot doesn't mean complete abandonment. Take Instagram's story of subtraction again. They began as a cluttered mix of check-ins, plans and photos. It was going nowhere. The founders didn't announce a big pivot. They didn't abandon social networking either – they just stripped everything except photos. That single act of subtraction turned a cluttered app into a global habit.

Mindset Cue: Big pivots thrill to win headlines. Micro decisions compound to win markets.

Micro decisions get powerful as they compound. A tweak in pricing brings in more users. More users generate better word-of-mouth. Better word-of-mouth attracts capital. Each move builds on the last. Momentum doesn't come from one pivot, but from the compounding of dozens of small, right calls.

For founders, the lesson is sharp. Don't wait only for grand pivot moments. Pay attention to the small choices – the product, the perception, the pricing, the innovation, the culture. These are the levers that, over time, tilt the entire company.

The Mindset Shift

Startups often fail when founders misread the moment. When they pivot out of fear. Or persist out of comfort.

The founder's job isn't to chase every craze. It's to stay tuned. To listen deeply to the market. To spot patterns, test small, decide with clarity, and act with courage.

This Adaptive Mindset is a founder's real muscle. It strengthens every time you drop ego, trust real signals, and commit fully. Every micro choice adds endurance. Stack enough of these choices, and you build resilience. Ignore them, and you are heading towards a collapse.

Success rarely comes from one defining moment. Not the viral feature, the dream pitch, or the dramatic pivot. It comes from dozens of small adaptive calls made over time because markets shift. Competitors close in. Customers evolve. Technology never pauses. *In this storm, foresight isn't your advantage. Adaptability is. Agility is.*

Nokia and Kodak missed it – and vanished. Instagram, Lenskart and Slack mastered it – and changed the game. No playbook lasts forever. But adaptability does.

15

The Scale Mindset

Expanding with Systems Thinking

Adaptability helps you survive. But survival isn't the goal, thriving is. To thrive, you need to scale, not through force, but with systems that grow naturally. That's the Scale Mindset.

Growth can feel intoxicating. New customers arrive, revenues climb, and the team races to keep pace. It appears to be momentum, but often it's merely acceleration without structure. What appears to be scaling may simply be stretching. And when you stretch too fast without reinforcement, things tend to collapse.

Founders often confuse 'more' with scalable. More sales, more hires, more features. But scale is not about piling up. Then what does the scale look like? A business truly scales when its systems absorb added load without breaking. When ten customers or ten thousand receive the same experience, when teams expand without culture dilution, when complexity rises, but chaos does not.

Hustle may fuel growth, but it cannot carry scale. Endless effort burns out. Sustainable scale demands a system design that makes growth repeatable, predictable and resilient.

Scale as Stability, Not Speed

Speed shines. But speed without stability is just momentum heading for a wall. Scale isn't about going faster. It's about pushing ahead without falling apart. That way, scale and growth are two different things altogether. Think of it like building a bridge. Growth is laying down more beams more quickly. Scaling is strengthening the bridge so it can handle more traffic without breaking because of fragility. True scale flips fragility into resilience. Growth hacks evolve as processes. Culture becomes a system. Technology turns into architecture.

Back in the 1990s, Amazon was just an online bookstore.[1] They could have only chased speed – selling more books, adding categories recklessly, pushing growth at all costs. Instead, Bezos obsessed over stability at scale. He poured into logistics, warehousing and cloud infrastructure that appeared oversized for the company's size back then.[2]

Those 'overbuilt' systems became Amazon's edge. When the dot-com bust wiped out competitors, Amazon's resilience kept it alive. Later, the same backbone powered Prime, AWS and its logistics empire. Amazon scaled not by sprinting the fastest but by building systems sturdy enough to carry unimaginable weight.

Now contrast this with how WeWork dealt with scale. They grew fast, expanding into city after city, chasing valuations, plastering their brand everywhere. But beneath the gloss, systems were brittle. Culture cracked under expansion. Operations were driven by hype, not stability. When market reality hit, growth turned into collapse. Back then, WeWork had speed, but no spine.

Systems Thinking: The Scale Stabiliser

> **Mindset Cue: Scale isn't about being the biggest or fastest. It's about designing for resilience before the weight arrives. Growth adds volume. Scale ensures you can hold it.**

Scale demands resilient processes and processes are forged by systems. And in a startup, 'system' is never about independent action in isolation. It is an interdependent web of operations in which products, teams, customers and capital constantly influence one another. Break one link, and the whole rhythm collapses. A world-class product with a weak onboarding system frustrates customers. A strong sales team with no reliable product loses trust. Generous funding without disciplined execution only accelerates the downfall. That's where systems thinking comes in.

Systems thinking is the founder's ability to see these hidden connections and patterns and design for harmony. It's not about solving problems in isolation. Instead, it's about shaping the whole ecosystem so that parts reinforce each other rather than collide.

Traditional problem-solving asks, what's broken and how do we fix it?

Systems thinking asks: *why does this problem keep happening, and how does it connect to the rest?*

Mindset Cue: Systems thinking is about thinking in loops and not lines.

When founders ignore systems, growth feels like a sprint – fast and aggressive, but short-lived. Teams burn out, customers leave, and decisions become reactive. But when a startup grows through systems thinking, it scales steadily. Progress compounds over time, and growth becomes smoother, more predictable and sustainable.

That's why companies like Zerodha scaled without spending crores on advertising. They integrated technology, trust and cost efficiency into a single ecosystem. Every operational saving lowered user fees, every loyal user brought in referrals, and every referral reduced acquisition costs. Thus it formed a cycle that grew without incurring cash outflows.

Founders with a systems mindset design startups like dynamic ecosystems – self-learning, self-correcting and scalable by design. They build loops that create compounding outcomes. Something like customer delight leads to referrals; referrals improve revenue predictability; predictability funds better talent; better talent improves the product; the loop continues.

Most founders are wired for action. They think in to-do lists and linear progress: launch product → acquire users → raise funds → hire team → scale. That's typical linear operator thinking.

But real growth is never linear. It's cyclic. What you fix in marketing affects sales; what you tweak in product changes support load, and what you decide in pricing impacts brand trust. To move from operator thinking to systems thinking, founders must adopt a mindset that calls for a pause and a zoom out. Instead of asking 'What's next?', they must ask 'What connects?'

That shift transforms decision-making from firefighting to architecture.

Mindset Cue: Systems thinking doesn't just optimise, it stabilises. It builds resilience into the company's DNA so that growth doesn't collapse under its own weight.

Amazon's flywheel model is a masterclass in system design. Each decision was a spoke in a reinforcing wheel: lower prices attracted more customers, more customers brought in more sellers, more sellers increased selection, better selection improved the customer experience, and that experience again attracted more customers. The wheel turned itself.

More recently, Notion nailed scale with systems thinking like no one else. It did not scale through ads or celebrity endorsements. It built a self-propelling system. The product's flexibility encouraged users to create templates. Those templates were shared on YouTube, Reddit and Twitter, acting as free marketing. The growing user community generated feedback that shaped faster product improvements. Better products led to more templates and even stronger communities. It was a loop – product, community and marketing feeding one another in harmony.

Here are some hands-on practices for founders to forge a Scale Mindset through systems thinking:

1. Zoom out before you react. When something breaks, don't fix it immediately. Map its connections. Figure out what else it touches. Often, the visible problem is just a symptom of a deeper imbalance in the system.

2. Replace KPIs with feedback loops. Instead of chasing isolated metrics ('user growth' or 'cost per lead'), design loops where improvements in one metric naturally strengthen others.
3. Design for stable growth, not a speedy one. Scaling fast without synchrony creates fragility. Scaling in rhythm builds endurance. Systems thinkers align speed with stability. Founders who master systems thinking move from controlling chaos to orchestrating flow. They stop asking, 'How do I grow faster?' and start asking, 'How do I make growth inevitable?'
4. Create structures that learn. Encourage your team to share patterns beyond wins and losses, paying attention, instead, to what connects them. Over time, this collective awareness becomes your company's nervous system.

Real scale doesn't come from isolated wins or hero moments. It arises from invisible systems quietly reinforcing each other – day after day, decision after decision.

That's the systems mindset – the hidden engine behind every scalable startup.

Repeatability: The Scale Driver

Startups often run on adrenaline. In the early days, it's the founder pulling all-nighters, chasing customers, fixing bugs, and closing deals. This kind of heroics works for survival, but it can never carry a company into scale. A business that depends on a founder's personal hustle is fragile. The moment the founder steps away, the engine stalls.

Real scale begins when outcomes don't depend on the intensity of individuals, but on the reliability of systems. When processes, not personalities, create results. When every customer interaction, delivery or support ticket has a rhythm that others can follow, regardless of who is running it.

McDonald's mastered this truth through design, not drama. In the 1950s, the McDonald brothers, Richard and Maurice, reimagined the kitchen as an 'assembly line for food'. From flipping patties to wrapping burgers, every movement was studied, timed and optimised. When Ray Kroc joined them, he saw not a restaurant, but a scalable system. He documented every process, built training manuals, created the Hamburger University to standardise learning, and ensured that every outlet from Chicago to Chennai delivered the same speed, taste and experience.

McDonald's didn't scale by selling more burgers. It scaled by training thousands of people to operate the same system with the same precision. It was discipline disguised as simplicity. Every detail engineered for consistency. Whether it was supplier contracts, store layouts or staff training, everything was designed to minimise variability and maximise control. That's what made the brand unstoppable.

Thus, scaling isn't about doing more of everything. It's about designing something once and making it work beautifully, again and again, anywhere in the world. Founders who fail to build repeatability stay trapped in a loop of crisis management. While those who embrace it build companies that grow even when they're not around to guide every decision.

The Founder's Shift: From Operator to Architect

In the beginning, founders do it all. They build, sell, support, pitch, and fix every problem that lands on their desk. That intensity is part of the startup foundation. But what drives early survival can't drive long-term scale. When a company's success depends entirely on a founder's solo grind, it's nothing but dependency. The moment the founder steps back, everything slows down.

To truly scale, founders must shift from being operators to becoming architects. The former fixes problems. The latter designs entire systems to ensure that problems don't repeat. Operators fight battles while architects design to win wars.

This shift isn't about doing less. It's about designing better. The right question changes from *'How do I fix this?'* to *'How do I design this so it doesn't need fixing yet again?'* That's systems thinking: creating self-sustaining mechanisms where each part strengthens the next.

In its early years, Melanie Perkins and her small team at Canva personally onboarded users, designed templates, handled support, and managed every feature request. But as millions joined the platform, that hands-on model couldn't keep up. Perkins realised she needed to stop being the problem-solver and start being the system designer.

So, she built systems that scaled without her. She created a product design framework in which every new feature followed a simple principle – 'empower the non-designer'. Moreover, she established team pods that owned specific user outcomes, rather than just tasks, ensuring every group could operate independently. She also invested early in data loops where every click, share and design action informed subsequent product decisions.

The result? Canva has scaled to over 180 million users across 190 countries without burning cash or losing simplicity. Perkins didn't scale by doing more. She scaled by designing systems that could do more without her.

That's the architect's mindset. Build systems that hold, even when you step aside.

Mindset Cue: The scale begins when systems, not people, bear the weight.

At times, an architect-founder steps back not to escape work, but to design how work happens. They turn delegation into design, and trust into structure. They stop fighting fires and start preventing them.

Founders who stay as operators stay stuck in daily chaos. Founders who think like architects build companies that grow and adapt on their own.

When Scale Fails

Scaling without systems is like building a skyscraper on sand. The taller it gets, the faster it crumbles. Many startups confuse early momentum with readiness to scale, only to realise that speed without structure makes them fragile, not fast.

The traps are familiar. Hiring too many people without a shared culture, chasing new markets before proving profitability, or launching new features faster than the system can support. Growth looks exciting until it collapses under its own weight.

BYJU'S symbolised India's startup dream for years.[3] A domestic company scaling globally, bringing digital education to millions, drawing the attention of the world. But beneath the headlines of valuations and acquisitions lay a fragile truth – BYJU'S mistook momentum as validation for scale.

Byju Raveendran built his empire on hustle. The company's early success came from aggressive sales-driven growth – thousands of feet on the street, daily targets, high-pressure conversions and a culture obsessed with speed. Every new market entered, every acquisition made, and every dollar raised was fuelled by relentless execution, not systemised design.

It worked for a while. The company's valuation surged past $22 billion, with over 40 acquisitions in under four years. But as revenue soared, cracks deepened. There were no unified operating systems binding the sprawl. Almost no cohesive integration of teams, technology, or culture. Each business unit operated in silos, and decisions often bottlenecked at the founder's table.

Instead of designing frameworks that could think, act and adapt independently, the organisation became dependent on the founder's individual vision and velocity as reported. When the market slowed, and scrutiny rose, the absence of scalable architecture became evident: unreconciled accounts, delayed audits, cultural fatigue and mass layoffs followed. BYJU'S wasn't weakened by a lack of ambition but by a lack of structure.

Systems thinking was missing. The company optimised for growth, not continuity. Its founder never transitioned from operator mode, solving problems faster than the system could learn from them.

Mindset Cue: It is the founder's job to build architectures before acceleration. Reinforce processes, governance, and decision rhythms that scale independently of the founders themselves.

The lesson? Hustle can build momentum. Architecture sustains it.

On the contrary, Zoom's story shows what happens when the opposite is done right.[4] Before the pandemic, Zoom wasn't the loudest player in video communication. Skype, WebEx and Google Meet dominated most headlines. But founder Eric Yuan was obsessed with one thing: reliability at scale. Every system was built to handle tremendous load – low latency across geographies, adaptive video compression for weak internet, cloud architecture that could spin up capacity instantly, and an interface simple enough for a child to use. Zoom wasn't chasing hype. It was quietly perfecting infrastructure and governance.

So when the pandemic surfaced and daily meeting participants jumped from 10 million to over 300 million in months, Zoom stretched but didn't shatter. It stumbled briefly with a security incident but adapted quickly, fixing flaws and reinforcing its core. The company's ability to absorb unprecedented demand wasn't luck. It was the outcome of years of system-first thinking. It was Yuan's choice to prioritise system architecture over growth acceleration. That's what a Scale Mindset looks like. And that's what most startups miss.[5]

Mindset Cue: Scaling isn't about speed. It's about stability under speed.

It's about designing operations, culture and technology so they can multiply gracefully. When systems are weak, scale brutally exposes cracks. But when systems are strong, scale compounds impact.

Every founder eventually faces this crossroads – scale chaos or scale clarity. Do you chase growth with hustle or build structure for endurance? Because growth can hide inefficiencies for a while, but scale always brings them to light.

In the end, scale doesn't forgive – it reveals. It multiplies whatever's underneath: discipline or disorder, systems or shortcuts.

The Compounding Effect of Systems

A well-built system works like compound interest. Steady, small improvements multiply results over time. Most founders think scale is about doing more – more features, more hires, more marketing. However, systems thinkers know that doing better compounds faster than doing more.

Think of your company like a flywheel. It doesn't need constant pushing. It needs intelligent design to sustain motion. When systems work predictably in onboarding, product delivery or decision-making, every new customer or team member strengthens momentum rather than slowing it.

When Groww started, India's investment platforms were complex, paperwork-heavy and intimidating. Instead of spending on massive sales teams, Groww built systems that simplified user onboarding to a few taps: instant KYC, an intuitive UI, and seamless bank integrations.

But the real compounding began behind the scenes. Every user action improved workflows such as fraud detection, personalised insights, and transaction reliability. The system didn't just handle scale; it learned from it. As user volume grew 100x, operations barely expanded. Each improvement in the efficiency fed the next, turning process design into a growth engine. Groww proved that compounding isn't just financial, it's structural.

> **Mindset Cue: When systems reduce friction, growth becomes self-fuelling.**

In an AI-first world, most companies scale by making models bigger and often break them in the process. Anthropic took a different route. Instead of chasing size, it focused on alignment. Its 'Constitutional AI' framework created a feedback system where models learn safely, predictably, and within clear rules. Each new version improves not because more people work on it, but because the system itself keeps getting better.

More users → better feedback → smarter models → more users – a self-improving loop that served as the strongest kind of compounding. Anthropic didn't grow through hype or brute force. It grew through architecture. It built systems that become more reliable with increased use.

Clearly, compounding doesn't come from hustle – it comes from structure. Essentially, once the founder's approach is set to identify, build and reinforce repeatable systems, the company scales autonomously. Because what repeats, compounds. And what compounds, scales.

IPO: Go or No-Go?

Scale is tested in many ways. You check for consistent profitability, durable market share, or a loyal user base that compounds over the years. An initial public offering (IPO) is the most public trial of scalability and systems.

An IPO is not the destination of scale. It is one of the possible checkpoints. Most companies will never go public, and that is fine. But for those who reach it, an IPO often becomes the sharpest mirror of this reality. Suddenly, your numbers are no longer internal dashboards. They are filed quarterly for the world to read. Your governance is not just about personal judgement; it is subject to regulatory scrutiny. Your story is not just told to investors in closed rooms. Analysts on live television dissect it. Numbers, governance, and growth stories are dissected quarter after quarter. If the foundation is weak, the market exposes it mercilessly.

Mindset Cue: Going public is not just about raising money. It's putting your systems under the harshest light of scrutiny.

Coinbase IPO is one of the world's largest crypto exchanges, built on the promise of making digital assets safe and accessible.[6] Before going public, it had already invested heavily in the systems that matter for a volatile industry – compliance, custody infrastructure, security, predictable revenue through transaction fees, and clean unit economics. These systems gave it stability in a market known for chaos.

By the time of its listing in 2021, Coinbase held a private valuation of about $68 billion. The IPO pushed that to $85+ billion on the first day because the market trusted the company's machinery. Even when crypto cycles later dipped, Coinbase didn't collapse; its operational core held. The IPO amplified what was already strong – trust, transparency and discipline.

Mindset Cue: When systems are sound, public markets don't scare you. They scale you.

CarTrade is an online marketplace for buying, selling and auctioning cars. On paper, it reached profitability before listing, but the internal systems that are critical to long-term scale (steady demand, marketplace liquidity, CAC efficiency and defensible growth engines) were not yet stable. Competition was rising, the used-car market was shifting, and the business didn't have enough repeatability to withstand public pressure.

CarTrade went public in 2021 at a valuation of approximately ₹7,500 crore, but the stock listed below its issue price on Day 1 and declined by almost 70 per cent within the first year. The moment public–market scrutiny arrived, every weak link – slow growth, loose governance and low-repeat behaviour – became visible. The IPO didn't fail because of the market alone; it failed because the company's internal systems weren't ready to compound at scale.

> **Mindset Cue: When the system isn't stable, an IPO doesn't multiply momentum; it magnifies fragility.**

An IPO is not a casual hunt for honour; it's a stress test of a company's scalability. Consequently, its timing should follow the readiness of internal systems, not the excitement of the moment. A startup is ready to go public when its processes run predictably, its numbers survive external audits, its governance is clean, and it can answer tough questions without fear. Going public should amplify your strengths, not hide your weaknesses.

Founders must avoid rushing to public markets when growth depends on hustle, not structure. Avoid it when unit economics are unstable, operations are inconsistent, or transparency will create panic. Public money cannot be used to fix private problems.

Scale works only when the system works. An IPO does not create sustainability. It reveals it.

The Mindset Shift

Scale isn't a race to get bigger – it's the discipline to get stronger as you grow. Startups that endure obsess over building foundations that can carry weight. Systems become their silent backbone. Without them, growth becomes shaky, and momentum collapses.

This is the real founder test – ignoring vanity growth and investing in the boring, essential plumbing that keeps the whole structure standing. Hustle fades, but systems compound. True scale is when the business runs, grows and adapts without you hovering over every decision. That's when you know you haven't just built a startup, you've built a system that can outlive you.

16

The Exit Mindset

Closing Chapters, Launching Legacies

EVERY STARTUP STORY HAS two endings. In one, the founder steps aside. In the other, the company steps forward.

Exits are not just transactions; they are strategic transitions. They mark the moment when a founder shifts roles. From builder to legacy holder. From operator to enabler of continuity. The venture that once leaned on you must now prove it can stand without you.

The uncomfortable truth is that most founders postpone this thought. They see exits as distant or irrelevant until a crisis, an irresistible offer, or investor pressure forces the decision. But founders who scale with foresight understand that exit was always part of the plan. It is not failure; nor is it escape. It is the natural arc of a system built to outlive its creator.

For instance, RedBus got acquired by Ibibo Group, yet the platform continued to grow and expand under new leadership. Or Little Eye Labs, a tiny Indian startup acquired by Meta, showing how even small teams can exit into global ecosystems. Or Mindtree, where founders gracefully stepped back after the L&T takeover, preserving the company's identity while letting new ownership steer the next chapter. Or WhatsApp, acquired by Meta – a billion-user platform whose founders eventually walked away when values no longer aligned.

Exits are punctuation marks in the story of a startup. A comma is when leadership passes hands. A semicolon is when the company merges into something bigger. A full stop is when the story concludes and closes for good.

An exit is the founder's final, conscious mic-drop – a move that must be made with clarity, calm and long-term intent. However, the timing is never fixed. It depends on a combination of personal goals, organisational strengths and market realities.

That's where the Exit Mindset steps in. It's not about walking away. It's about choosing the moment when the company can walk on its own. It's the mindset that forces three hard questions every founder must confront: *does my company survive without me? And does my legacy live beyond me? Is this the right time?*

Why Exits Matter

All founders celebrate beginnings, but few plan endings. Yet every venture, no matter how ambitious, eventually faces one. Exits are not only about liquidity. They are about continuity. They decide whether a company matures into an institution or fades into memory.

A well-designed exit largely shapes three things. First, *the company's future*, ensuring products, teams, and customers continue to thrive even if the founder steps aside. Second, *the founder's legacy* that defines how the builder is remembered, say as a creator of enduring value or as someone who left too soon. Lastly, *the system's continuity* so that tested and established systems remain relevant inside future ecosystems. A thoughtful exit strengthens that system, not weakens it.

Think of YouTube's acquisition by Google.[1] It wasn't just a payout. It was an act of survival. Without Google's infrastructure and legal muscle, YouTube may have collapsed under bandwidth costs and copyright battles. The exit gave it life beyond its founders. Or consider LinkedIn's sale to Microsoft. Again, not out of desperation but out of clear foresight. As part of Microsoft, LinkedIn scaled faster while keeping its identity intact. The exit was not an end; it was an expansion. All these exits are rooted in the founder's well-measured strategy aiming to offer larger or better continuity to their ventures.

Exits matter because they reveal the truth of what was built – a founder's individual hustle or a system that can continue to thrive without the one. They allow you to design business continuity or reinfuse life and survival into the business against market shifts. Every exit tells a different story – shaped by the reason behind it, the timing chosen, and the outcome it creates for both the founder and the business.

Forms of Exit

Exits come in many shapes. Some arrive with applause, some with silence, and some with the hard lessons of failure. But every exit leaves a trace of the founder's decisions, the team's grit, and the vision that drove it.

One of the most common is the *strategic exit* when a bigger player steps in, not just for your revenues, but for your edge. This could be your product, your customers, or your team. It's the kind of exit where your creation becomes part of a larger story. Nest Labs was a strong smart-home startup in its own right. But once it joined Google, it became part of a much bigger vision for connected living. That's what a strategic exit does. You don't just sell; you scale on a larger platform.

Mindset Cue: A strategic exit forces a simple choice: is your product intended to stand alone or become part of a larger system? Founders who choose the latter can let go without losing pride.

Then there's the *financial exit*, where the focus is on liquidity. This is when founders, investors and early believers finally convert their stake into real returns. It could be an IPO, a secondary sale, or an acquisition driven mainly by shareholder value. LinkedIn's $26 billion sale to Microsoft is a clear example. Stakeholders saw a major payout, and the product entered a new chapter under a broader tech umbrella.

A financial exit demonstrates that the value built over the years can be realised in a single moment. But what happens to the product afterwards depends on who's behind the steering wheel. It confirms that what was built was real, but it doesn't write the legacy. Every founder must reflect on this: am I chasing a momentary reward, or building something that endures?

Sometimes the product doesn't make it, but the people do. That's a *talent exit*, often termed as an acqui-hire. Big companies like Meta, Nvidia and Tesla often absorb small teams whose products didn't scale but whose skills matter. Dozens of AI, gaming and design startups have taken this route. The startup brand disappears, yet its core competence finds new life within a larger organism. It's not the story most founders dream of, but it's still a way of ensuring the work and talent live on.

Mindset Cue: A talent exit requires humility. Your creation may not have scaled, but your team did. True founders recognise the value in letting the team continue, even if the startup doesn't.

Not every exit means stepping out entirely. A *partial exit* is a balancing act that allows founders to partially cash out, reduce personal risk, and remain involved. It's a way to let go of what's no longer driving growth while holding on to what still matters. Paytm followed this path with Paytm Mall – pulling back on one part while the larger company continued forward. This exit requires a founder to answer the question: what do I need to retain for control, and what can I relinquish for clarity?

And then there's the *legacy exit* – steady, quiet and often overlooked because it doesn't come with big announcements or bold moves. Here, the founder doesn't sell; instead they step back. Succession becomes the plan for handing leadership to the next generation or to capable captains. Infosys is a classic example. Its founders transitioned out gradually, allowing the company's culture and values to outlive their personal involvement. Legacy exits may not dominate headlines, but they often create the most enduring impact. A legacy exit asks one simple question. Will the company stand strong without you? It's not about cashing out. It's about ensuring continuity beyond your presence.

Finally, there's the exit most founders fear – *the shutdown*. Sometimes the market shifts, competition intensifies, the runway dries up, or the product simply can't keep pace. Closing down is painful, but it's still an exit – one that leaves behind lessons for the ecosystem. Founded as India's WhatsApp rival, Hike became a unicorn with 100M+ users before shutting its messaging app in 2021 due to WhatsApp's network dominance. It pivoted to real-money gaming with Rush, gaining strong traction. But India's 2025 ban on real-money gaming dismantled its core model, leading founder Kavin Bharti Mittal to opt for a global shutdown instead of pursuing a costly regulatory reset. Hike's eventual closure became a powerful lesson in market dominance, timing and the brutal vulnerabilities of consumer tech. However, a shutdown isn't the end of the founder's ambition; it's a reset that forces honesty and clears space for the next chapter.

Mindset Cue: A shutdown demands courage. It's the hardest exit to accept, but often the most honest. Sometimes closing a venture is not a failure. It's making room for the founder's next, truer beginning.

Exits aren't just transactions, not just business events. They are tough decisions about what to continue and what to conclude. And that demands a resilient yet agile and conscious mindset. Whether it's strategic, financial, legacy or even a shutdown, every exit pushes a founder to confront the same core truth – how does this story carry forward without me? Ultimately, your exit becomes the version of your startup that the world remembers.

The Founder's Dilemma: When to Step Aside

The hardest question in the founder's journey is when to let go. Timing an exit demands both courage and clarity. Too early, and you miss what the company could have become. Too late, and momentum slips through your fingers. Once hailed as India's edtech poster boy, Byju Raveendran's reluctance to recalibrate leadership and step back in time eventually turned into a cautionary tale of the collapse of a $22 billion unicorn.

Exits aren't just financial decisions; they are human ones. When a founder's energy dips, the company feels it. Knowing when to step aside is a sign of clarity, not failure. History is full of founders who overstayed. Some clung to control, only to watch their vision get diluted by crisis. Others left with precision, setting their companies free to scale without friction.

Take Howard Schultz of Starbucks. He didn't just leave once and disappear; he stepped away when the company was stable, returned when the brand started drifting from its core values, and finally exited when the operational and leadership systems were strong enough to sustain growth without him. For Schultz, timing was about stewardship and responsibility, not personal ego or wealth. His exit ensured the company continued to thrive, with its culture and strategy intact, long after he had formally left the CEO role.

Contrast that with Travis Kalanick of Uber. Kalanick's early brilliance and relentless hustle built a global ride-hailing empire, but as the company scaled, the systems and governance needed to support it lagged. His hands-on style and aggressive approach, once a strength, became a liability in a complex global operation. The board had to step in. His exit was forced rather than voluntary. The lesson is clear. Staying too long

Mindset Cue: The right exit comes when the systems are mature, the culture is intact, and the business can thrive without you. Clearly not when ego or circumstance forces the decision.

without scaling yourself into the system can put both the founder and the venture at risk.

As startups grow, roles evolve faster than founders do. The intuition and innovation skills that spark a company aren't always the ones that help it mature. Somewhere between early chaos and steady scale lies a difficult crossroads: the moment when a founder must decide whether to leave or stay to lead the next chapter. That's the founder's dilemma in its most vulnerable form: 'Should I stay because I can still add real value? Or am I staying simply because I can't imagine myself outside this story?'

It's a question that shapes both your legacy and your company's future. And this is where the inner test begins. A simple, clarity-driven framework – **VRS** – can cut through the noise and dilemma:

'V' stands for *Vision Test*. Does your personal vision for the company still align with where the market is heading? If your dream feels smaller than the opportunity, the company needs new leadership to match its horizon.

'R' stands for *Role Test*. Are you still the best person for the job today? The scrappy hustler who thrives in chaos may not be the right fit for disciplined global execution. If you're forcing yourself into a role you don't enjoy, it's a signal.

'S' stands for *System Test*. Can the company function without you? If every decision still funnels through you, the system isn't ready. True readiness for exit occurs when the machine continues to run even if the operator steps out.

Founder's Dilemma: Stay or Go?

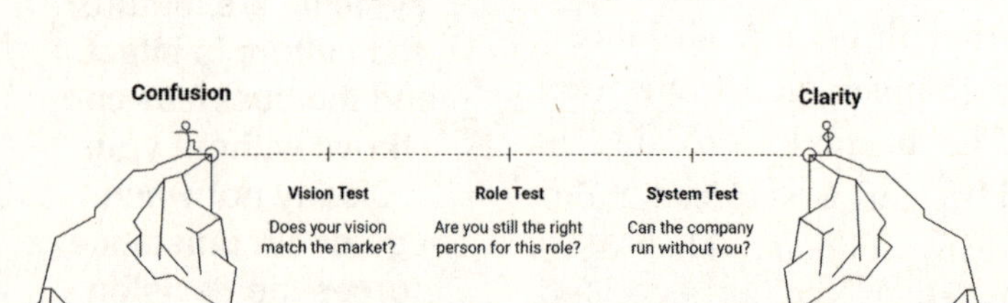

If a founder answers no to these three tests, the message is obvious. Staying on isn't leadership, it's fear. This is the moment to trade attachment for clarity. To shift focus from your presence to the company's endurance. Instead of 'Am I ready to leave?' the real question becomes 'Is the company ready to stand on its own?'

Designing for Continuity

An exit is not the end. It is a handoff. The company must not stumble the moment the founder leaves. Continuity is the true legacy. However, the harsh reality remains that many startups fade when the founder steps back. Not because the idea was weak, but because the founder never built a system beyond themselves. The strongest founders build companies that breathe on their own. They embed culture into habits. They install processes that make decisions predictable without killing creativity. They shape a bench of leaders who don't just follow orders but advance the vision.

As Bryan Miles rightly quotes, 'If your company dies with you, you didn't build a company. You built a job.' The founder's true victory is when the company grows stronger in their absence.

Look at Apple. When Steve Jobs passed away, sceptics believed Apple would collapse without his vision. Yet Apple thrived under Tim Cook. Not because Jobs was replaceable, but because he had already designed a culture of obsession with detail, innovation pipelines and leadership depth. Continuity was baked into the DNA.

Something similar happened with Microsoft. Bill Gates gradually stepped back, handing the reins to professional leadership. Decades later, Satya Nadella could reshape Microsoft into a cloud-first powerhouse because systems and succession were strong. The company didn't lose its soul. It evolved.

Info Edge, the company behind classifieds such as Naukri, 99acres, Jeevansathi and others, is yet another masterclass in continuity. Sanjeev Bikhchandani built not just products but also an ecosystem of leaders and ventures.[2] Even as he withdrew from day-to-day operations, the company thrived, backed by institutional strength, disciplined governance, and a portfolio designed for long-term relevance.

To administer continuity like these champion corps, every founder must master three deliberate acts broadly.

First, *codify the culture.* A founder's energy is contagious, but culture cannot sustain only in high-octane motivational townhalls created by the founder. It needs to be codified in rituals, practices and principles that shape everyday behaviour. If the company can't tell you what it stands for without mentioning your name, it isn't ready.

Second, *build leadership layers.* A startup grows through concentric circles of leadership. If every key decision still comes back to the founder, there's no layer. Mentoring a second line is not optional; it is insurance. The goal is simple: make yourself replaceable.

Third, *create operating systems.* Beyond culture and people lies structure. Repeatable processes, decision frameworks and governance rules that keep the company steady even when personalities change. The stronger the operating system, the smoother the transition.

Mindset Cue: Continuity is about humility. It is about accepting that the company is not your personality cult. It is an organism larger than you.

Exits Shape Ecosystems

An exit is never just a company's story. It ripples outwards. It shifts industries. It inspires founders. It attracts capital. It builds confidence in entire ecosystems. The way a founder exits often creates more impact than the way they entered.

Let's understand this through three groundbreaking exits. Each one didn't just close a chapter; it opened new ones and set off waves of change.

Take Instagram. Facebook bought it in 2012 for $1 billion. Critics dismissed the deal: a photo app, 13 employees, too pricey. But the ripple was huge. It made mobile-first, visual-first the new norm. Proven small, scrappy teams could out-innovate giants. Facebook gave Instagram fuel to become a global cultural force. One exit. The consumer internet was never the same.

When PayPal was sold to eBay in 2002, it wasn't a closing chapter. It was the catalyst for what followed. The PayPal Mafia didn't slow down; they went on to build Tesla, SpaceX, YouTube, LinkedIn and Palantir.[3] One exit created a network of capital, talent and ambitious ideas. Exits don't just reward founders. They multiply them. They seed the next generation of builders.

Similar to PayPal's landmark exit, Flipkart's exit brought an unprecedented transformation.[4] A single exit boosted the startup landscape for the entire Indian subcontinent. When Walmart acquired it for $16 billion in 2018, it signalled that India was ready for world-class startups. A company that began in a small apartment had grown big enough to attract the world's largest retailer. That exit changed everything. Investor confidence in India shot up. Young founders now believed they could build at global scale without leaving the country. Second-time founders emerged in large numbers. The 'Flipkart Mafia' took shape – former leaders went on to build Udaan, Groww, Navi, Curefit and dozens more. Even PhonePe, born inside Flipkart, matured and eventually became its own giant.[5] Culture, skills and playbooks spread across the ecosystem. One exit didn't just reward founders, it lifted an entire generation of Indian startups.

Some exits are quieter, yet just as powerful. Apple's buying of Beats wasn't about headphones. It unlocked Apple Music. Info Edge's early bet and partial exits from Zomato showed Indian investors could nurture and repeat success.

Each exit exceeded the deal sheet. They shaped behaviour, capital flows and founder courage. They shifted what people believed was possible. They expanded the playing field for everyone who followed.

Mindset Cue: Exits aren't endings. They're tectonic shifts. Done right, they don't just change one company. They change the future of ecosystems.

When Exits Go Wrong

While exits are milestones, not all of them shine. Some exits are remembered less for the wealth they created and more for the lessons they left behind. The harshest form of exit is the *fire-sale.* It happens when a company runs out of options – no cash, no clear path, and investors desperate to recover scraps. The founder's dream gets sold not for the vision, but for liquidation.

Yet another more brutal exit is *culture-kill.* Startups are more than products. They are tribes built on energy, belief and founder spirit. When absorbed by a larger corporation, this culture often dies. The product may survive, but the purpose vanishes. Look at Zappos under Amazon. Zappos was legendary for its 'Delivering Happiness' ethos, nurtured by Tony Hsieh. But years under Amazon's operational weight diluted its identity. Employees reported that the spark had faded, and customers noticed the difference.

As an exit, IPO often seduces founders as the ultimate milestone. But only after a while, you get to know that the public market is unforgiving. And you can't jump just like that. A startup may soar on hype, but without solid numbers, the descent is swift. What's meant to be an exit becomes a cautionary tale. Zomato's IPO was celebrated and oversubscribed as a symbol of India's digital leap. However, within months, the stock halved as profitability concerns became evident. Zomato eventually rebuilt credibility, but that first stumble made investors wary. That said, unlike Zomato, numerous IPOs never bounce back, they wither under public scrutiny and disappear.

Sometimes, exits fail not at the deal, but afterwards. Poor integration between the acquirer and the acquired leads to product stagnation, talent drain and customer churn. In 2013,

Yahoo bought Tumblr for $1.1 billion, hoping to reinvent itself with youth appeal. Within a few years, Tumblr was written down to nearly nothing.

When exits go wrong, the damage is more than financial. Founders walk away disillusioned. Employees feel betrayed. Ecosystems lose confidence.And damage becomes irreversible. As noted previously, exits aren't merely transactions; they're transformations.

Mindset Cue: Money without meaning leaves scars. And legacy without alignment collapses.

Every exit leaves a mark. Sometimes that mark shows up in numbers. Sometimes it shows up in stories. Money fades, valuations fade, but the impact your company leaves on people, markets and culture lasts much longer. And that's legacy. Take Freshworks. Its Nasdaq listing lit a fire in India's SaaS community. Early team members are now funding and building new ventures. A founder's truest legacy often isn't the product they built, it's the people they empowered to build after them.

Sometimes, legacy shows up as a signal. When Naukri went public in 2006, it wasn't only raising funds, it was raising confidence. It quietly told Indian founders: 'Internet startups can make it to the public markets.' That one moment became a milestone for an entire generation.

So the term 'legacy' isn't just about how big you grow. It's about the imprint you leave behind – the ripple, the mindset, the new doors you open. Money may start the spark, but legacy is the fire that keeps burning.

The Legacy Champion: Tata

A legacy that survives generations is never an accident. It doesn't come from quarterly targets or viral moments. It emerges from a long-term vision, sustained discipline and the ability to adapt. Many founders chase the next pivot or funding round. Very few think about what will remain when they are gone. Tata did.

For more than 150 years, the Tata Group has navigated changing markets, emerging technologies and multiple leadership transitions. Yet its core purpose has stayed steady. It's a story of leadership that outlasts individuals, systems that stay strong in turbulence, and decisions that shape decades.

When Jamsetji Tata founded the company in 1868, it began as a simple cotton trading business. But his vision was far larger than profit. He dreamed of steel plants, electric power and institutions of learning. Tata Steel and the Indian Institute of Science stand today as proof of one simple truth: a lasting legacy begins with long-term vision.

Across generations, Tata endured leadership exits and successions, acquisitions and mergers, launches and closures. From Jamsetji to Dorabji, JRD, Ratan Tata and N. Chandrasekaran, every leader to date exhibits the same leadership DNA in ethos, mindset and decision-making. Whether it is about launching a venture, acquiring a company, or shaping culture, every next step is still weighed for cross-generational impact. Systems form the nucleus of Tata's enterprises. Each company runs independently yet stays connected. Risks are distributed, governance is structured, and processes are disciplined. That's why Tata absorbs leadership changes, market shocks and global disruptions without losing its identity.

Tata championed adaptability right from its inception. The group shifted from textiles to steel, automobiles, IT, chemicals, hospitality and renewable energy – always observing the market, pivoting carefully, deciding decisively, and committing fully. Not every venture turned a profit. The Tata Nano didn't, yet it symbolised the leadership's audacity and intent.

Tata's brands carry the quiet promise of reliability with responsibility. TCS grew into a global IT powerhouse. Tata Motors made mobility accessible to millions. Tata Salt and Taj Hotels became symbols of trust in homes and hearts.

Strategic moves, such as the acquisition of Jaguar Land Rover, protected the legacy while unlocking new growth. And when Air India returned to the group in 2022, it was history coming full circle.

Beyond its entrepreneurial structure, philanthropy remains central to Tata. Over 60 per cent of Tata Sons's equity fuels charitable trusts advancing education, healthcare and social change. Tata personified the view that profit is a means, not an end. Exits and growth serve society as much as shareholders.

Tata's story unveils how growth must be seen beyond balance sheets in the trust truly embedded across generations. For founders, the exits are opportunities to ensure continuity. Tata demonstrates that when you focus on purpose, responsibility and resilience, your venture can transcend time. Exits become a milestone, not a finale. And the founder's journey doesn't end there. It continues to be reinvented, amplified, and forever linked to the ecosystem it built.

Not every founder can, or needs to, build Tata. However, every founder must aspire to build with purpose and exit, leaving a lasting legacy.

The Mindset Shift

Exits are the ultimate test of a founder's vision. Building for continuity matters as much as building for growth. The right exit, at the right time, protects culture, strengthens the ecosystem, and leaves a legacy far deeper than profits. Because legacy is about creating something that lasts, inspires and uplifts. A founder's journey doesn't end at the exit door. It evolves. One chapter concludes, and another begins – with new roles, new impact and new possibilities waiting on the other side.

Acknowledgements

Behind every written word stands an unwritten influence. This book, too, is the outcome of many such influences that have shaped my vision over the years.

My foremost and deepest gratitude goes to my spiritual master, H.H. Radhanath Swami Maharaj, whose life and teachings instilled in me the value of sharing. In spirit, much of what is articulated in these pages draws from that foundation.

To my family, my parents, whose sacrifices built the ground I stand on, and whose quiet strength made every risk feel less reckless. To my wife, Dr Meenu Chauhan, for offering her unwavering support, thoughtful challenges and the quiet resilience that strengthened this journey. And to my son, Hanu, whose gentle yet persistent reminders became an unexpected discipline system. This manuscript owes them more than it may ever express.

To the founders, mentees and coworkers in the ecosystem who trusted me with their journeys. Your stories, struggles and breakthroughs are the spine of this work. Whatever is useful in these pages was tested in your trenches first.

I am grateful to my friend and publisher Manish Khurana and the team at Bloomsbury India for their patience and professionalism. The form I envisioned for this book demanded unusual flexibility, and it was carried with remarkable ease across unconventional timelines.

My gratitude to Dr Rohit Khokar, for his unconditional belief and support in taking this work to leaders and communities beyond boundaries.

And finally, I duly acknowledge the failures, setbacks and obstacles that served as the most exacting teachers. Whatever clarity this book offers has been shaped less by success and far more by everything that didn't work out.

Appendix 1
The Founder's Financial Discipline Matrix

Pillar	What It Means	Founder's Actions*	Thumb Rule*
Cashflow Vigilance	*Understanding cash in and out movements and avoiding contingencies.*	*Roll a 12-month cashflow sheet and track inflow vs commitments monthly.*	*Minimum 12–18 months runway before the next capital event.*
Burn Rate Discipline	*Knowing how much the startup burns monthly and where.*	*Audit team, infra and marketing spends quarterly.*	*Healthy burn = ≤ 15–20 per cent of available cash / month.*
CAC–LTV Logic	*Ensuring the cost to acquire a customer justifies their lifetime value.*	*Track CAC, LTV, churn, payback time.*	*LTV ≥ 3 × CAC, Payback ≤ 12 months.*
Capital Allocation Strategy	*Planning to distribute available capital for measurable outcomes.*	*Assign budgets to growth levers and keep eye on ROI.*	*70 per cent core ops, 20 per cent innovation, 10 per cent contingency*
Founder Pay and Lifestyle Balance	*Setting salary and lifestyle in sync with the company stage.*	*Fix founder pay at sustainability level, not luxury.*	*Founder pay = 10–15 per cent of total fixed cost or market median.*
Fundraising Timing	*Raising funds before desperation, after validation.*	*Map capital needs 9–12 months ahead or more.*	*Raise when the traction curve is rising, not when it is flat.*
Frugality vs. Scarcity	*Spending smartly without a scarcity mentality.*	*Invest in efficiency tools and systems. Skip vanity spends.*	*Frugality = ROI-driven spending, not withholding.*

Pillar	What It Means	Founder's Actions*	Thumb Rule*
Profit Path Clarity	*Knowing when and how the model turns profitable.*	*Define profit milestones early. Monitor gross margin.*	*Break-even visibility within 24–30 months.*
Financial Reporting	*Keeping financial health visible and updated.*	*Monthly P&L and cashflow review. Quarterly board reporting.*	*Review reports every 30 days.*
Scenario Planning	*Preparing for shocks (market, burn, delay).*	*Build base, best- and worst-case financial models.*	*Maintain three scenarios with action triggers.*
Debt vs. Equity Discipline	*Knowing when to borrow and when to dilute.*	*Use debt for predictable revenue streams only.*	*Maintain Debt-to-Equity ≤ 0.3 at seed.*
Financial Learning Loop	*Continuously building financial acumen.*	*Attend finance discourses. Decode investor reports.*	*Minimum two hours/week on financial learning.*

* Founder's actions and thumb rules shared herein are generic guidelines and thus must be administered keeping in view the particular startup context.

Appendix 2

The Metric Menu: Founders' Financial Toolkit

Metric	What It Is	Why It Matters	How to Optimise
Gross Margin	*Revenue kept after direct costs*	*Fuels ops, growth and profit.*	*Improve pricing, cut direct costs, shift to higher-margin products*
Contribution Margin	*Cash earned after variable costs.*	*Shows true per-unit profitability.*	*Reduce variable costs, bundle/upsell, optimise fulfilment.*
Unit Economics	*Profitability per customer/unit over payback.*	*Determines if scaling creates or destroys cash.*	*Improve CAC efficiency, raise contribution margin, shorten payback.*
CAC	*Cost to acquire each customer.*	*High CAC kills runway and payback.*	*Optimise channels, improve funnel, cut expensive acquisition sources.*
LTV	*Net value earned from a customer over time.*	*Defines sustainable CAC and growth.*	*Improve retention, increase repeat purchase, add upsells.*
EBITDA	*Operating profit before non-cash items.*	*Core health of the business*	*Tighten costs, improve efficiency, lift gross margins.*
EBITDA Trend	*Direction of operational performance.*	*Early signal of improvement or decline.*	*Fix margin leaks, control overheads, adjust pricing.*

Metric	What It Is	Why It Matters	How to Optimise
Burn Rate	*Monthly net cash outflow.*	*Dictates speed of cash depletion.*	*Cut non-essentials, plan hiring, renegotiate expenses.*
Runway	*Cash in bank ÷ Monthly Net Burn, or simply months before cash runs out.*	*Drives fundraising and cost decisions.*	*Reduce burn, boost revenue, plan to fundraise timely.*
PAT	*True bottom-line after all expenses.*	*Shows real profitability.*	*Improve margins, manage overheads, plan taxes well.*
Cohort Contribution	*Profitability tracked by customer cohorts.*	*Reveals payback and retention quality.*	*Fix churn points, improve onboarding, double down on strong cohorts.*
Gross vs Net Burn	*Gross signifies total outflow while net signifies outflow , minus inflows.*	*Gross signals discipline. Net points runway.*	*Monitor both, remove recurring leaks, manage inflows better.*

* Metrics menu shared herein offers generic guidelines. Administer, keeping in view your particular startup context.

Appendix 3
Startup References Index

S. No.	Startup	Founder(s)	Chapter(s)	Key Manoeuvres
1	*Airbnb*	*Brian Chesky, Joe Gebbia*	*Chapter 2* *Chapter 4* *Chapter 10* *Chapter 13* *Chapter 14*	*Sold Obama O' s cereal during 2008 crisis to raise $40K. Survived funding crisis, validated market through direct action, host interviews, visits before scaling to a $100B company.*
2	*Amazon*	*Jeff Bezos*	*Chapter 2* *Chapter 5* *Chapter 15*	*Started with books, then studied customer data for expansion signals. Strategically diversified to AWS, cloud services, transformed into a $1T conglomerate.*
3	*Anthropic*	*Dario Amodei, Daniela Amodei*	*Chapter 15*	*Built Constitutional AI frameworks prioritising system architecture over model size. Designed a system that improves itself and strengthens its competitive moat without piling on more features.*

S. No.	Startup	Founder(s)	Chapter(s)	Key Manoeuvres
4	*Basecamp*	*Jason Fried, David Hansson*	*Chapter 12*	*Built a simple project management tool. Charged from Day 1. Targeted small businesses. Stayed intentionally small and profitable. Grew users steadily. Played the long game.*
5	*Beats*	*Dr. Dre, Jimmy Lovine*	*Chapter 16*	*Positioned Beats as a brand ecosystem and not just headphones, with Apple Music integration. Apple acquired for $3B and unlocked Apple Music's music streaming dominance.*
6	*BYJU'S*	*Byju Raveendran*	*Chapter 13* *Chapter 15* *Chapter 16*	*Measured course completion rates and quiz engagement as growth metrics. Optimised content, learning outcomes and scaled the model successfully. Growth was founder-led and so was the collapse under governance issues.*
7	*Calendly*	*Tope Awotona*	*Chapter 10* *Chapter 12*	*Reinvested revenue into the product. Stayed focused. Reached millions of daily users.* *Built consistent profitability first and then raised $350M at a $3B valuation in early 2021 for acceleration. Scaled enterprise sales. Launched advanced AI scheduling. Expanded into Europe and Asia.*

S. No.	Startup	Founder(s)	Chapter(s)	Key Manoeuvres
8	*Canva*	*Melanie Perkins*	*Introduction Chapter 2 Chapter 3 Chapter 15*	*Faced 100+ rejections but doubled down on testing over polishing pitches. Built a design–democratisation company valued at $40B. Now a benchmark in founder resilience.*
9	*Clubhouse*	*Paul Davison, Rohan Seth*	*Chapter 11*	*The social audio platform raised approx. $112 million in early funding. Hit unicorn valuation pre product–market fit. Scaled on hype. No durable engagement. Retention lagged investor expectations. Capital magnified the execution gaps.*
10	*Coinbase*	*Brian Armstrong, Fred Ehrsam*	*Chapter 15*	*Invested heavily in compliance, custody, security infrastructure before pursuing rapid growth. Surviving multiple crypto crashes while competitors failed, it became the first major crypto IPO.*
11	*Color Labs*	*Bill Nguyen*	*Chapter 3 Chapter 11*	*Raised $41M, launched product without deep understanding of photo-sharing user behaviour. Engineered virality that didn't resonate. The product failed despite massive capital and execution.*

S. No.	Startup	Founder(s)	Chapter(s)	Key Manoeuvres
12	*Curefit*	*Mukesh Bansal, Ankit Nagori*	*Chapter 16*	*Flipkart employees took learnings from exit, applied systems thinking to new verticals like Fitness. Built successful venture, validated that founder exits spawn multi-venture ecosystems.*
13	*Dehaat*	*Shashank Kumar, Harsh Songra*	*Chapter 10*	*Founders built from lived experience. Solved a problem they grew up with. Targeted broken farm supply chains. Earned trust through authenticity. Credibility became moat.*
14	*Dropbox*	*Drew Houston*	*Chapter 2* *Chapter 4*	*Created a three-minute explainer video to validate demand before building a full product. Demonstrated demand signal. De-risked $1M raise. Became SaaS validation playbook.*
15	*Dunzo*	*Kabeer Biswas*	*Chapter 9* *Chapter 11*	*Raised via WhatsApp screenshots at angel stage, then structured micro-rounds. Stretched runway for more than three years. Forced disciplined unit economics to survive.*

S. No.	Startup	Founder(s)	Chapter(s)	Key Manoeuvres
16	*Duolingo*	*Luis von Ahn, Severin Hacker*	*Chapter 6* *Chapter 7* *Chapter 8* *Chapter 14*	*Stayed focused on gamified learning, used a freemium model, hired for mission fit, raised strategically. Sequential mindset mastery created compounding advantage; scaled to 500M+ users.*
17	*Evernote*	*Stepan Pachikov*	*Chapter 3*	*Added messaging, tasks, collaboration features beyond core note-taking. Lost product focus. Caused user confusion. Innovation slowed. Company value declined over time.*
18	*Fab.com*	*Jason Goldberg, Nishith Shah*	*Chapter 5*	*Hit $1B valuation, immediately expanded to 100+ cities globally without validating unit economics locally. Weak retention, massive burn. The company died despite strong initial traction.*
19	*Facebook*	*Mark Zuckerberg, Eduardo Saverin, Dustin Moskovitz, Chris Hughes*	*Chapter 13*	*Invented the playbook. Played cross-functional. Treated growth as a product problem, not a marketing campaign. Scaled from millions to billions.*

S. No.	Startup	Founder(s)	Chapter(s)	Key Manoeuvres
20	*Figma*	*Dylan Field, Evan Wallace*	*Chapter 10*	*Began with no heavy product-led pitching. Led with one line: 'Design together, in the browser.' Simplified a complex category. Challenged bulky desktop incumbents. Made collaboration the hook. Tested the pitch in meetups and dorm rooms. Refined through real conversations. Simplicity carried conviction.*
21	*FirstCry*	*Supam Maheshwari*	*Chapter 1*	*Started in the wedding gifting market. Saw customer data showing stronger interest in baby products. Pivoted entirely. Now India's largest baby platform with $100M+ revenue.*
22	*Flipkart*	*Sachin Bansal, Binny Bansal*	*Chapter 8* *Chapter 16*	*Distributed ₹3,500+ crore to employees via ESOP during Walmart exit. Exit built the Flipkart Mafia ecosystem. Ex-executives spawned Udaan, Groww, Curefit, PhonePe as $10B+ ventures.*

S. No.	Startup	Founder(s)	Chapter(s)	Key Manoeuvres
23	*Freshworks*	*Girish Mathrubootham, Shan Krishnasamy*	*Chapter 7* *Chapter 16*	*Kept lean structure and scaled with product. Monetised via tiered upgrades. Guarded burn and churn. Extended runway to $500M+ ARR on discipline. Pursued Nasdaq IPO (2021) over early acquisition offers. Signalled to Indian SaaS founders that public-market scale is possible. Unlocked investor conviction in SaaS ventures.*
24	*Google Glass*	*Google*	*Chapter 5*	*Executed brilliant engineering. Ignored market feedback about discomfort, privacy concerns, social awkwardness. Product rejected by market. Billions wasted on brilliant execution of a wrong problem.*
25	*Groww*	*Lalit Keshre, Harsh Jain*	*Chapter 15* *Chapter 16*	*Simplified KYC, focused on frictionless UI, integrated banks. Deliberately omitted non-core features. Scaled 100x with the same operational headcount. Became a $12B+ Unicorn fintech platform.*

S. No.	Startup	Founder(s)	Chapter(s)	Key Manoeuvres
26	*Hike*	*Kavin Mittal*	*Chapter 16*	*Challenged the WhatsApp's dominant network. Scaled to unicorn velocity. Faced structural vulnerabilities. Pivoted into gaming to build monetisation. Built traction again. Faced regulatory disruption. Refused prolonged uncertainty. Opted for decisive closure.*
27	*Hopin*	*Johnny Boufarhat*	*Chapter 13*	*London-based virtual event and conferencing platform. Rode pandemic surge. Raised at peak momentum. $8 billion valuation in less than two years. Scaled headcount globally. Acquired aggressively. Mistook temporary demand for durable behaviour. Faced contraction when pandemic normalised.*
28	*Housing. com*	*Rahul Yadav*	*Chapter 2* *Chapter 11*	*Burned $100M+ recklessly on hiring, marketing, luxury offices without a validated revenue model. Investor trust eroded. Forced founder exit. Capital became liability instead of advantage.*

S. No.	Startup	Founder(s)	Chapter(s)	Key Manoeuvres
29	*HubSpot*	*Brian Halligan, Dharmesh Shah*	*Chapter 13*	*Built a systematised inbound engine with a repeatable funnel – from content to lead magnets, free tools and paid subscriptions. Every stage was measured, optimised, and documented, unlocking consistent, predictable growth.*
30	*Instagram*	*Kevin Systrom, Mike Krieger*	*Chapter 1 Chapter 4 Chapter 13 Chapter 14 Chapter 16*	*Abandoned Burbn and 500K users within weeks after recognising photo-sharing signals. Pivoted entirely. Launched Instagram. Multiplied on a single feature: photo-sharing. Reached 100M users in two years. Acquired by Facebook for $1B in 2012.*
31	*Info Edge*	*Sanjeev Bikhchandani*	*Chapter 16*	*Pursued 2006 public listing as first major Indian internet IPO. Signalled to founders 'internet startups can reach public-market scale in India'. Unlocked an ecosystem-wide founder confidence.*
32	*Kuku FM*	*Lal Chand Bisu, Vikas Goyal*	*Chapter 11*	*Raised angel capital on thesis 'next billion users won't speak English' despite VC scepticism. Built vernacular audio platform. Proved non-obvious TAM. Now $500M+ company.*

S. No.	Startup	Founder(s)	Chapter(s)	Key Manoeuvres
33	*Kodak*	*George Eastman*	*Chapter 14*	*Feared venturing into the digital era. Leadership remained stuck to the old film photo. Shelved the breakthrough idea. Entered the digital space late. Lost the battle to Sony and Canon.*
34	*Lenskart*	*Piyush Goyal*	*Chapter 11* *Chapter 14*	*Began online, soon realised the trust barrier, added at-home eye check-ups and trials. Expanded into offline retail as 'omnichannel' retailer. Pivot in channel, not product.*
35	*LinkedIn*	*Reid Hoffman*	*Chapter 13* *Chapter 16*	*Used constant A/B testing in its early years to refine user engagement. Derived multipliers from growth experiments. Later, negotiated Microsoft acquisition at $26.2B with post-exit autonomy clause. Maintained product independence post-acquisition. Continued innovation as the world's largest professional network.*
36	*Mailchimp*	*Ben Chestnut, Dan Kurzius*	*Chapter 12*	*Generated early revenue through freemium plans to fund product enhancements to pull more paid users. Profits cycled back into features, creating a flywheel that helped Mailchimp grow into a marketing powerhouse without a single VC penny.*

S. No.	Startup	Founder(s)	Chapter(s)	Key Manoeuvres
37	*Meesho*	*Vidit Aatrey*	*Introduction Chapter 13*	*Started with WhatsApp groups of 500+ sellers targeting non-urban India. Listened to actual user needs. Built a billion-dollar platform. Validated that grit applied to authentic needs beats polished pitches.*
38	*McDonald's*	*Richard McDonald, Maurice McDonald, Ray Kroc*	*Chapter 15*	*Standardised every movement, every recipe, every layout. Engineered repeatability. Systemised the kitchen. Launched Hamburger University to institutionalise training. Engineered supplier control. Designed stores for precision. Turned a restaurant into a replicable operating system.*
39	*Navi*	*Sachin Bansal, Ankit Agarwal*	*Chapter 16*	*Used ₹5,600 crore Flipkart exit capital to build a fintech venture in a new vertical. Demonstrated founder optionality post-exit. Proved exits can launch next-generation entrepreneurship.*

S. No.	Startup	Founder(s)	Chapter(s)	Key Manoeuvres
40	*Netflix*	*Reed Hastings*	*Chapter 2* *Chapter 14*	*Bet the entire company on streaming. Then disciplined investment in original content. Transformed entertainment. Now worth $250B. Showed thoughtful dare and patient execution beats quick wins.*
41	*Notion*	*Ivan Zhao, Simon Last*	*Chapter 3* *Chapter 15*	*Product designers solved their own tool-switching pain daily. Built for themselves first. More a decade years to profitability but authentic fit. Now $10B+ valuation. Validated that right-fit compounds. Nailed scale with self-propelling system thinking like no one else.*
42	*OYO*	*Ritesh Agarwal*	*Chapter 10* *Chapter 11*	*Began lean with a blend of micro-traction and macro-vision. Grew exponentially city by city. Raised $2B+ and expanded thousands of properties globally but without validating unit economics locally. Burn caught up. Massive layoffs, restructuring. Demonstrated that undisciplined mega-funding brings the reckoning sooner.*

S. No.	Startup	Founder(s)	Chapter(s)	Key Manoeuvres
43	*PayPal*	*Peter Thiel, Elon Musk*	*Chapter 16*	*Sold to eBay for $1.5B. Founders distributed capital to build next ventures. Spawned PayPal Mafia (LinkedIn, YouTube, Tesla, Palantir, SpaceX, Yelp). $500B+ in value created post-exit.*
44	*Paytm*	*Vijay Shekhar Sharma*	*Chapter 1* *Chapter 6* *Chapter 8* *Chapter 16*	*Visioned mobile payments before 4G. Stayed focused on UPI. Built fail-fast teams. Positioned for exit. Became a unicorn exemplar for the Indian ecosystem. Proved sequential mindset mastery builds trajectory.*
45	*Pets.com*	*Not specified*	*Chapter 5*	*Raised $300M. Burned on Super Bowl ads, free shipping without validated unit economics. Internet crash poster-child. Filed bankruptcy in two years. Showed execution excellence can't rescue flawed model.*
46	*PhonePe*	*Sameer Nigam, Rahul Chari*	*Chapter 16*	*Incubated inside Flipkart but turned out as an independent venture. Focused vertically on payments. Became India's largest payments platform. Demonstrated that tight focus lets such spin-offs surpass their parent.*

S. No.	Startup	Founder(s)	Chapter(s)	Key Manoeuvres
47	*Piramal Group*	*Dr Swati Piramal, Ajay Piramal*	*Chapter 2*	*Sold a successfully running pharmaceutical business in 2010. Pivoted to healthcare analytics, real estate, fintech. Recognised end of pharma cycle. Repositioned for the future. Proved daring includes disrupting legacy for opportunity.*
48	*Quibi*	*Jeffrey Katzenberg, Meg Whitman*	*Chapter 5* *Chapter 8* *Chapter 13*	*Raised $1.75B. Launched premium short-form content, massive marketing without market validations. Surrounded by yes-men. Shut down in six months proving that execution excellence and capital mean nothing without product–market fit.*
49	*Razorpay*	*Harshil Mathur, Shashank Kumar*	*Chapter 9* *Chapter 10* *Chapter 13*	*Started with one sharp focus, i.e. seamless online payment acceptance. Built developer-first APIs. Simplified onboarding. Removed integration friction. Supported founders directly. Hired top talent early. Raised micro-rounds with controlled dilution. Maintained tight capital discipline. Reached ~30% market share in six years. Proved steady scaling beats blitz funding.*

S. No.	Startup	Founder(s)	Chapter(s)	Key Manoeuvres
50	*Shopify*	*Tobias Lütke, Scott Lake*	*Chapter 4*	*Launched with core features like checkout, payments, etc. Deliberately omitted non-core features. Iterated via real merchant feedback. Became e-commerce infrastructure. Today a $200B+ company.*
51	*Slack*	*Stewart Butterfield*	*Chapter 5* *Chapter 10* *Chapter 14*	*Gaming platform Glitch failed. But the internal communication tool showed real engagement. They pivoted fully, launched Slack, and became the global workplace standard. Proved that spotting the wrong problem early beats blindly persisting with the thesis.*
52	*SpaceX*	*Elon Musk*	*Chapter 6*	*Stayed focused on reusable rockets. The market called that impossible. Trusted physics over market consensus. Achieved reusable rocket technology proving that real founders sometimes must ignore markets.*
53	*Spanx*	*Sara Blakely*	*Chapter 1*	*Started with $5K. Faced repeated retail rejections. Tested prototypes on self. Built conviction through iteration. World's youngest self-made female billionaire, proving resilience compounds into scale.*

S. No.	Startup	Founder(s)	Chapter(s)	Key Manoeuvres
54	*Spotify*	*Daniel Ek, Martin Lorentzon*	*Chapter 13*	*Founded in 2016. A Swedish audio streaming and media service provider. Early on, optimised for one core metric, i.e. listening time as North Star Metric. Aligned every team. Prioritised habit over downloads. Designed for repeat sessions. Compounded attention. Focused on time spent. Turned engagement into moat.*
55	*Starbucks*	*Howard Schultz*	*Chapter 2* *Chapter 16*	*Bet career on premium coffee culture when coffee was commodity. Created $100B+ category. It dared to see value in future categories, not just optimising current ones.*
56	*Stripe*	*Patrick Collison, John Collison*	*Chapter 11* *Chapter 13*	*Founders faced the early failure, visited customers, sat with them, and installed Stripe themselves. The 'Collison installation programme' turned legendary. A founder-led growth hack that made Stripe spread like wildfire.*
57	*Teachmint*	*Mihir Gupta, Payoj Jain, Divyansh Bordia, Anshuman Kumar*	*Chapter 11*	*Raised $20M+ on transparent metrics (clear CAC, LTV). No growth theatre. Built investor conviction faster. It proved that capital mindset means founder transparency in metrics.*

S. No.	Startup	Founder(s)	Chapter(s)	Key Manoeuvres
58	*Tesla*	*Elon Musk*	*Chapter 2* *Chapter 6* *Chapter 14*	*Dared on EVs. Focused on the energy ecosystem. Scaled via systems thinking. Stayed independent. Seventeen-year long journey building $1T+ company proving sequential mindset mastery creates generational impact.*
59	*TinyOwl*	*Harshvardhan Mandad, Gaurav Choudhary, Shikhar Paliwal, Saurabh Goyal, Tanuj Khandelwal*	*Chapter 11*	*Raised capital aggressively. Expanded operations at high speed. Chased app installs through heavy discounts. Failed to build product stickiness. Overloaded logistics with premature scale. Lost users when incentives stopped. Collapsed despite raising over $27M.*
60	*Theranos*	*Elizabeth Holmes*	*Chapter 5*	*The founder chose yes-men over real men. Lacked scientific grounding in leadership. Executed elite strategy on false premise. Criminal fraud charges. It proved that elite execution of false premises accelerates towards legal liability.*
61	*Trello*	*Joel Spolsky, Michael Pryor*	*Chapter 13*	*Emphasised user consistency as a core metric. Tracked engagement. Refined the product around those behaviours, ensuring users stayed active long after sign-up.*

S. No.	Startup	Founder(s)	Chapter(s)	Key Manoeuvres
62	*Tumblr*	*David Karp*	*Chapter 16*	*Yahoo acquired for $1.1B. Didn't negotiate post-acquisition autonomy or culture preservation. Written down to $20M. Culture dismantled, ads imposed. It proved that exits fail on integration, not price alone.*
63	*Twitter*	*Jack Dorsey*	*Chapter 5*	*A failing podcast platform, Odeo saw its future in internal micro-posting. The full pivot created Twitter and a new layer of social infrastructure proving that execution mastery is the courage to pivot boldly.*
64	*Udaan*	*Amod Malviya, Sujeet Kumar*	*Chapter 16*	*Founders (ex-Flipkart executives) applied exit learnings to the new vertical, B2B commerce. Built $2B+ company. It proved that mega-exits spawn founder networks and legacy compounds through talent distribution.*
65	*WeWork*	*Adam Neumann*	*Chapter 7* *Chapter 15*	*Locked into long leases, sold short-term rentals, and burned billions. The $47B peak vanished at IPO showing how flawed models inflate rapidly when funding outpaces fundamentals.*

S. No.	Startup	Founder(s)	Chapter(s)	Key Manoeuvres
66	*WhatsApp*	*Jan Koum, Brian Acton*	*Chapter 16*	*Secured a $19B deal with a strict no-ads condition, then red flagged acquirer Meta when it was broken. A reminder that iconic exits are driven by values first, valuation second.*
67	*YouTube*	*Chad Hurley, Steve Chen, Jawed Karim*	*Chapter 14 Chapter 16*	*Started as a dating site where people could upload short clips about themselves. Failed. Pivoted with a small adjustment. Opened the platform to any kind of video.*
68	*Zappos*	*Tony Hsieh*	*Chapter 16*	*Amazon acquired it for $1.2B. Didn't negotiate culture preservation, and the 'Delivering Happiness' ethos got diluted. Competitive edge lost. It proved that exits fail if integration destroys core assets.*
69	*Zepto*	*Aadit Palicha, Kaivalya Vohra*	*Chapter 10*	*Entered a crowded grocery delivery market. Observed a post-pandemic shift toward instant gratification. Positioned ten -minute delivery as feasible, not gimmicky. Made quick commerce credible to users and investors.*

S. No.	Startup	Founder(s)	Chapter(s)	Key Manoeuvres
70	*Zerodha*	*Nithin Kamath, Nikhil Kamath*	*Chapter 2* *Chapter 8* *Chapter 12* *Chapter 15*	*Dared to redefine discount broking. Built a lean team. Scaled profitably. It proved that bold bets need operational leanness – without it, they collapse into fiction.*
71	*Zoho*	*Sridhar Vembu*	*Chapter 17* *Chapter 12*	*Founded 1996. Rejected VC. Invested in product, user forums, and developer meetups to build organic growth. Maintained profitability from Day 1. Built HQ in rural Tamil Nadu. Clocked $1B+ revenue, still independent. Proven money mindset implies choosing capital discipline over venture acceleration.*
72	*Zomato*	*Deepinder Goyal, Pankaj Chaddah*	*Chapter 6* *Chapter 11* *Chapter 14* *Chapter 16*	*Started with reviews and stayed focused. Managed equity across multiple rounds and positioned for an exit. Became a unicorn, showing how single-minded mastery creates compounding advantage and true exit optionality.*
73	*Zoom*	*Eric Yuan*	*Chapter 15*	*Prioritised reliability architecture pre-launch. Built for 10x growth before the market signalled 3x demand. Scaled 10M to 300M users during Covid gracefully. Proven systems precede scale.*

Notes

Introduction

1 'It Took Melanie Perkins 100+ Rejections over 3 Years (& Some Faith!) to Give Life to Design Platform Canva', *Economic Times*, 13 July 2022. Available online: https://economictimes.indiatimes.com/magazines/panache/it-took-melanie-perkins-100-rejections-over-3-yrs-some-faith-to-give-life-to-design-platform-canva/articleshow/92845505.cms (accessed August 2025).

2 'Meesho: A Masterclass in New Category Creation', *Elevation Capital*, Available online: https://www.elevationcapital.com/stories/meesho-story (accessed August 2025).

1 The Foundation Mindset

1 D. Sweeney, '4 Great Lessons in Entrepreneurship Everyone Can Learn from Spanx Founder Sara Blakely', *Forbes*, 26 August 2018. Available online: https://www.forbes.com/sites/allbusiness/2018/08/26/entrepreneurship-lessons-spanx-founder-sara-blakely/ (accessed January 2025).

2 S. Maheshwari, 'FirstCry: Meet the Man Behind a Baby Business That Grew into a Giant', *Economic Times*, August 2024. Available online: https://economictimes.indiatimes.com/industry/services/retail/firstcry-meet-the-man-behind-baby-business-that-grew-into-a-giant/articleshow/112202021.cms (accessed March 2025).

3 A. Gautam, 'Paytm's Vijay Shekhar Sharma Revolutionised Digital Payments When Cash Was King', *NDTV*, 6 February 2024. Available online: https://www.ndtv.com/india-news/paytm-vijay-shekhar-sharma-rbi-paytm-wallet-paytms-vijay-shekhar-sharma-5003661 (accessed August 2025).

4 Elevation Capital, 'Paytm Story'. *Elevation Capital*. Available online: https://elevationcapital.com/stories/paytm-story (accessed August 2025).

2 The Dare Mindset

1 'The Simple Theory That Led to Netflix's Media Takeover', Nasdaq, 17 June 2018. Available online: https://www.nasdaq.com/articles/

simple-theory-led-netflixs-media-takeover-2018-06-17 (accessed December 2024).

2 P. Sareen, 'The Rise and Fall of Housing's Rahul Yadav', *Inc42*, 2 July 2015. Available online: https://inc42.com/buzz/rahul-yadav-timeline/ (accessed August 2025).

3 B. Bostock, 'Elon Musk Has Started Building a Tesla Gigafactory in China, and It Could Let Him Dodge Trump's Trade War', *Business Insider*, 7 January 2019. Available online: https://www.businessinsider.com/elon-musk-starts-telsa-gigafactory-in-shanghai-may-dodge-trump-trade-war-2019-1 (accessed December 2024).

4 N. Sood, 'Transformations, Pivots, and More: How Focusing on Change Helped Piramal Group Evolve and Grow (Leadership Talk Between Shraddha Sharma and Ajay Piramal)', *YourStory*, September 2021. Available online: https://yourstory.com/2021/09/transformations-pivots-change-evolution-piramal-group-growth (accessed January 2024).

3 The Right-Fit Mindset

1 M. Zhang, 'Photo-Sharing App Color Shutting Down, Sold for $7M After Raising $41M', *PetaPixel*, 20 November 2012. Available online: https://petapixel.com/2012/11/20/photo-sharing-app-color-shutting-down-sold-for-7m-after-raising-41m/ (accessed March 2024).

2 M. Finnerty, 'Notion CEO Ivan Zhao: Augmenting Human Intellect', *Sequoia Capital*, 13 October 2022. Available online: https://sequoiacap.com/article/notion-spotlight/ (accessed March 2024).

3 P. Hong, 'The Rise and Fall of Evernote: A Tale of Ambition, Innovation, and Change', *Founder Foundry*, 4 February 2025. Available online: https://www.founderfoundry.com/article/the-rise-and-fall-of-evernote-a-tale-of-ambition-innovation-and-change (accessed September 2025).

4 M. Perkins, 'The Woman Behind Canva Shares How She Built a $42B Company from Nothing', *Lenny's Podcast*, 2 November 2025. Available online: https://www.lennysnewsletter.com/p/the-making-of-canva (accessed November 2025).

4 The Action Mindset

1 P. Prakash, 'Airbnb's CEO Says a $40 Cereal Box Changed the Course of the Multibillion-Dollar Company', *Fortune*, 18 April 2023. Available online: https://fortune.com/2023/04/19/airbnb-ceo-cereal-box-investors-changed-everything-billion-dollar-company/ (accessed June 2024).

2 R. Hoffman, 'Be a Platform, with Shopify's Tobi Lütke', *Masters of Scale,* 4 April 2023. Available online: https://mastersofscale.com/episode/tobi-lutke-be-a-platform/ (accessed June 2024).

5 The Execution Mindset

1 J. Boorstin, 'Quibi Officially Announces It's Shutting Down', *CNBC*, 21 October 2020. Available online: https://www.cnbc.com/2020/10/21/quibi-to-shut-down-after-just-6-months.html (accessed August 2024).

2 'How DropBox Started As a Minimal Viable Product', *TechCrunch*, 19 October 2011. Available online: https://techcrunch.com/2011/10/19/dropbox-minimal-viable-product/ (accessed June 2024).

3 T. Dunn and V. Thompson, 'Ex-Theranos Employees Describe Culture of Secrecy at Elizabeth Holmes' Startup: "The Dropout" Podcast Ep. 1', *ABC News*, 12 March 2019. Available online: https://abcnews.go.com/Business/theranos-employees-describe-culture-secrecy-elizabeth-holmes-startup/story?id=60544673 (accessed August 2024).

4 A. Shontell, 'The Tech "Titanic": How Red-Hot Startup Fab Raised $330 Million and Then Went Bust', *Business Insider*, 6 February 2015. Available online: https://www.businessinsider.com/how-billion-dollar-startupstartup-fab-died-2015-2 (accessed August 2024).

5 L. Lulia, 'Why Demolition Man, Fab.com's Former CEO Should Have Studied TOM (at GSB) Before Running His Company into the Ground – Technology and Operations Management', *Harvard Business School*, 9 December 2015. Available online: https://d3.harvard.edu/platform-rctom/submission/why-demolition-man-fab-coms-former-ceo-should-have-studied-tom-at-gsb-before-running-his-company-into-the-ground/ (accessed March 2025).

6 U. Haque, 'Google Glass Failed Because It Just Wasn't Cool', *Harvard Business Review*, 30 January 2015. Available online: https://hbr.org/2015/01/google-glass-failed-because-it-just-wasnt-cool (accessed March 2025).

6 The Focus Mindset

1 C. Anderson, 'Elon Musk: A Future Worth Getting Excited About | Tesla Texas Gigafactory Interview | TED', *TED Podcast*, 18 April 2022. Available online: https://www.youtube.com/watch?v=YRvf00NooN8 (accessed October 2024); C. Anderson, 'Elon Musk: A Future Worth Getting Excited About | Tesla Texas Gigafactory Interview | TED', *Podcast Notes*, 18 April 2022. Available online: https://podcastnotes.org/ted-interview/elon-musk-ted/ (accessed October 2024).

2 S.N. Joni, 'Help Yourself and Help the World: An Interview With Duolingo CEO Luis von Ahn', *Forbes*, 30 May 2014. Available online: https://www.forbes.com/sites/forbesleadershipforum/2014/05/28/help-yourself-and-help-the-world-an-interview-with-duolingo-ceo-luis-von-ahn/ (accessed October 2024).

7 The Money Mindset

1 M. Harmon, 'WeWork: From Unicorn to Bankruptcy', *Harvard Business Review*, 17 September 2025. Available online: https://hbsp.harvard.edu/product/F323-PDF-ENG (accessed December 2024).

2 'If You Don't Invest in R&D, You Won't Have Long-Term Growth, Says Zoho Corp's Boss Sridhar Vembu', *Business Today*, 28 May 2023. Available online: https://www.businesstoday.in/magazine/interview/story/if-you-dont-invest-in-rd-you-wont-have-long-term-growth-says-zoho-corps-boss-sridhar-vembu-381656-2023-05-17 (accessed January 2025).

8 The Team Mindset

1 'Luis von Ahn, Co-Founder and CEO of Duolingo — How to Be (Truly) Mission-Driven', *Tim Ferriss Show*, 14 July 2022. Available online: https://tim.blog/2022/07/12/luis-von-ahn/ (accessed March 2025).

2 '12 Operating Principles That Shape Our Innovative Culture', *Duolingo*, 1 December 2023. Available online: https://blog.duolingo.com/operating-principles/ (accessed March 2025).

3 Supraja Srinivasan and Madhav Chanchani, 'Walmart's Acquisition of Flipkart Rakes in $500m Moolah for Flipsters', *Economic Times*, 10 May 2018. Available online: https://economictimes.indiatimes.com/news/company/corporate-trends/walmarts-acquisition-of-flipkart-rakes-in-500m-moolah-for-flipsters/articleshow/64103252.cms. https://economictimes.indiatimes.com/news/company/corporate-trends/walmarts-acquisition-of-flipkart-rakes-in-500m-moolah-for-flipsters/articleshow/64103252.cms (accessed April 2025).

4 'From the Ground Up: Nithin Kamath & Rajan Anandan on Zerodha's Journey', *Peak XV*, 19 November 2024. Available online: https://www.peakxv.com/video/from-the-ground-up-nithin-kamath-rajan-anandan-on-zerodhas-journey/ (accessed October 2025).

5 Deepsekhar Choudhury, 'At the End of the Day, You Bet on Founders', *Outlook Business*, 2 February 2025. Available online: https://www.outlookbusiness.com/magazine/nithin-kamath-interview-at-the-end-of-the-day-you-bet-on-founders (accessed October 2025).

9 The Equity Mindset

1 Chandra Srikanth, 'Breaking Down Razorpay's Original Pitch with Harshil Mathur', *Seedtoscale Podcast*, 17 July 2025. Available online: https://www.seedtoscale.com/podcast/breaking-down-razorpays-original-pitch-with-harshil-mathur/ https://www.youtube.com/watch?v=5O28Or455Es (accessed August 2025).

2 'Razorpay: India's Only Full-Stack Financial Solutions Platform for Businesses', *Y Combinator*, 2022. Available online: https://www.ycombinator.com/companies/razorpay (accessed August 2025).
3 Jaryd Hermann, 'How Atlassian Grows', *HowTheyGrow.co*, 8 March 2023. Available online: https://www.howtheygrow.co/p/how-atlassian-grows (accessed August 2025).
4 Jordan Novet, 'How Atlassian's Dual-CEO Structure Has Helped the Company Thrive', *CNBC*, 31 March 2022. Available online: https://www.cnbc.com/2022/03/31/how-atlassians-dual-ceo-structure-has-helped-the-company-thrive.html (accessed August 2025).
5 'BharatPe, Ashneer Grover End Long-Drawn Courtroom Battle: The Story So Far', *Economic Times*, 26 September 2025. Available online: https://economictimes.indiatimes.com/tech/technology/bharatpe-ashneer-grover-end-long-drawn-courtroom-battle-the-story-so-far/articleshow/113808308.cms (accessed September 2025).
6 Anushka De, 'Ashneer Grover Severs All Ties with BharatPe Following Legal Settlement', *NDTV*, 30 September 2024. Available online: https://www.ndtv.com/india-news/ashneer-grover-severs-all-ties-with-bharatpe-following-legal-settlement-6681739 (accessed August 2025).

10 The Story Mindset

1 Aadit Palicha and Rajiv Srivatsa (Antler), 'How Zepto Made 10 Min Grocery Delivery Possible', *Neon.Fund Podcast*, 17 January 2024. Available online: https://neon.fund/podcasts/how-zepto-made-10-mins-grocery-delivery-possible-in-india-at-scale-with-founder-ceo-aadit-palicha/ (accessed August 2025).
2 Amy Feldman, 'Nigeria-Born Tope Awotona Poured His Life Savings into Calendly. Now He's One of America's Wealthiest Immigrants', *Forbes*, 6 April 2022. Available online: https://www.forbes.com/sites/amyfeldman/2022/04/06/nigeria-born-tope-awotona-poured-his-life-savings-into-calendly-now-hes-one-of-americas-wealthiest-immigrants/ (accessed September 2025).
3 Omer Khan and Tope Awotona, 'Calendly Founder Tope Awotona: Product-Market Fit After 3 Failed Startups', *SaaS Club Podcast*, March 2025. Available online: https://saasclub.io/podcast/calendlys-founder-finding-saas-success-after-failed-startups/ (accessed September 2025).
4 'From 0 to 1B: Slack's Founder Shares Their Epic Launch Strategy', *First Round Review*, February 2024. Available online: https://review.firstround.com/from-0-to-1b-slacks-founder-shares-their-epic-launch-strategy/ (accessed August 2025).
5 Andrew Warner and Ritesh Agarwal, 'OYO's One Change Made Billions', *Mixergy*, July 2023. Available online: https://mixergy.com/interviews/oyo-with-ritesh-agarwal/ (accessed September 2025).

6 'From College Dropout to Billion-Dollar Founder | Ritesh Agarwal on Building OYO India's Startup Boom', *MyGov India*, 8 March 2025. Available online: https://www.youtube.com/watch?v=5OwSUxUsi_s (accessed September 2025).

11 The Capital Mindset

1 Aparna Ghosh, 'TinyOwl's Downward Spiral: From Foodies' Favourite to Employees' Nightmare', *YourStory*, 4 November 2015. Available online: https://yourstory.com/2015/11/tinyowl-downward-spiral (accessed July 2025).

2 Rashmi Menon, 'The Rise and Fall of TinyOwl: Lessons That Start-Up Founder Saurabh Goyal Learnt', *Economic Times*, 15 August 2017. Available online: https://economictimes.indiatimes.com/magazines/panache/the-rise-and-fall-of-tinyowl-lessons-that-startup-founder-saurabh-goyal-learnt/articleshow/60069036.cms (accessed July 2025).

3 Sharddha S. and Deepinder Goyal, 'Zomato: The Inside Scoop', *YourStory*, 28 August 2017. Available online: https://yourstory.com/2017/08/zomato-deepinder-goyal-interview (accessed August 2025).

4 Mohit Bhatnagar, 'Zomato IPO: Re-imagining the Future of Food', *Peak XV*, 22 July 2021. Available online: https://www.peakxv.com/article/zomato-ipo-re-imagining-the-future-of-food/ (accessed August 2025).

5 Patanjali Pahwa, 'How Housing.com Tripped', *Business Standard*, 21 December 2015. Available online: https://www.business-standard.com/article/companies/how-housing-com-tripped-115122100028_1.html (accessed August 2025).

6 Sohini Mitter, 'Why Nandan Nilekani's Venture Fund Is Doubling Down on Kuku FM', *The CapTable*, 9 October 2023. Available online: https://the-captable.com/2023/10/nandan-nilekani-venture-fund-kuku-fm-audio-ott/ (accessed July 2025).

7 Rahul Sanghi, 'A Sonic Bridge to India's Heartlands: The Story of KukuFM', *Tigerfeathers*, 21 July 2023. Available online: https://www.tigerfeathers.in/p/a-sonic-bridge-to-indias-heartlands (accessed July 2025).

8 Manish Singh, 'Indian Edtech Teachmint Raises $20 Million to Expand to New Categories and Geographies', *TechCrunch*, 7 July 2021. Available online: https://techcrunch.com/2021/07/07/indian-edtech-teachmint-raises-20-million-to-expand-to-new-categories-and-geographies/(accessed July 2025).

9 Sandeep Soni, 'Amid OYO's Mass Layoffs, Founder Ritesh Agarwal Explains Firings; Full Text of Letter to Staff', *Financial Express*, 14 January 2020. Available online: https://www.financialexpress.com/business/sme-amid-oyos-mass-layoffs-founder-ritesh-agarwal-explains-firings-full-text-of-letter-to-staff-1821706/ (accessed August 2025).

12 The Bootstrap Mindset

1 Sahil Khanna and Nithin Kamath, 'Building a Profitable Bootstrapped Startup Like Zerodha', *YouTube*, 10 June 2022. Available online: https://www.youtube.com/watch?v=EfspH4au99s (accessed September 2025).

2 'Zerodha CEO Nithin Kamath Shares Tips for Bootstrapping Start-Ups, Says Not Every Business Can Scale', *Economic Times*, 14 June 2022. Available online: https://economictimes.indiatimes.com/magazines/panache/zerodha-ceo-nithin-kamath-shares-tips-for-bootstrapping-startups-says-not-every-business-can-scale/articleshow/92196709.cms (accessed September 2025).

3 Rob Walling and Ben Chestnut, 'How Ben Chestnut Bootstrapped Mailchimp to a $12 Billion Exit', *MicroConf US*, 12 May 2024. Available online: https://www.youtube.com/watch?v=jUyRLWSjarA (accessed September 2025).

4 Greg Head and Jason Fried, 'Why Jason Fried Never Took VC Money (and Never Will) | Zero to $10m Podcast', *Zero to $10m Podcast*, 9 January 2025. Available online: https://www.youtube.com/watch?v=O7_MwaVAG8s (accessed September 2025).

5 Courtney Connley, 'Why This Tech CEO Turned Down Funding from More Than 100 Investors', *CNBC*, 15 August 2017. Available online: https://www.cnbc.com/2017/08/15/why-this-tech-ceo-turned-down-funding-from-more-than-100-investors.html (accessed September 2025).

13 The Traction and Growth Mindset

1 Shounak Banerjee, 'From Bootstrapped to a $425 Million Exit: The Trello Story', *Marketcurve*, 26 February 2024. Available online: https://marketcurve.substack.com/p/from-bootstrapped-to-a-425-million (accessed May 2024).

2 Thomas J. Steenburgh and Jill Avery, 'HubSpot: Inbound Marketing and Web 2.0', *Harvard Business School*, January 2011. Available online: https://www.hbs.edu/faculty/Pages/item.aspx?num=37327 (accessed May 2024).

3 Brian Halligan and Dharmesh Shah, 'Official Flywheel Documentation', *HubSpot*, 7 September 2018. Available online: https://www.hubspot.com/flywheel (accessed May 2024).

4 Thomason Rajan, 'The Unusual Case of BYJU's: Creating One of the World's Most Valued Educational Technology Companies from India', *Indian Journal of Entrepreneurship*, 15 April 2022. Available online: https://www.indianjournalofentrepreneurship.com/index.php/ijom/article/download/163181/115682 (accessed June 2025).

14 The Adaptive Mindset

1 Joe Gebbia and Phin Barnes, 'How Design Thinking Transformed Airbnb from a Failing Startup to a Billion Dollar Business', *First Round Review*. Available online: https://review.firstround.com/how-design-thinking-transformed-airbnb-from-failing-startup-to-billion-dollar-business/ (accessed May 2024).

2 M.G. Siegler, 'A Pivotal Pivot: Instagram Story', *TechCrunch*, 8 November 2010. Available online: https://techcrunch.com/2010/11/08/instagram-a-pivotal-pivot/ (accessed June 2025).

3 Karthik B. Reddy and Peyush Bansal, 'Peyush Bansal of Lenskart Talks About Clarity of Purpose, Customer Obsession, and Culture', *Blume Ventures Podcast*, 2 August 2023. Available online: https://blume.vc/podcasts/blume-podcast/peyush-bansal-of-lenskart-talks-about-clarity-of-purpose-customer-obsession-and-leading-with-culture (accessed June 2025).

4 Kartik Kapahi, 'Omni Channel: Seamless Post-Sales Experience', *Lenskart Official Blog*, 18 April 2021. Available online: https://blog.lenskart.com/omni-channel-seamless-post-sales-experience-5304c220a921 (accessed June 2025).

5 Jon Russell, 'Restaurant Discovery Site Zomato to Launch Food Delivery Service, Starting in India', *TechCrunch*, 11 February 2015. Available online: https://techcrunch.com/2015/02/11/zomato-food-delivery/ (accessed July 2025).

6 Chunka Mui, 'How Kodak Failed', *Forbes*, 17 January 2012. Available online: https://www.forbes.com/sites/chunkamui/2012/01/18/how-kodak-failed/(accessed July 2025).

7 Kasper Karlsson, 'The Dilemma That Brought Down Kodak', Quartr, 21 August 2025. Available online: https://quartr.com/insights/edge/the-dilemma-that-brought-down-kodak (accessed September 2025).

8 Jorma Ollila, 'Nokia Downturn: Ex-CEO Ollila Concedes Mistakes', *Arab News*, 18 October 2013. Available online: https://www.arabnews.com/news/468046 (accessed September 2025).

15 The Scale Mindset

1 John R. Wells and Benjamin Weinstock, 'Amazon.com, 2021', *Harvard Business School*, June 2021. Available online: https://www.hbs.edu/faculty/Pages/item.aspx?num=49324 (accessed September 2025).

2 Sunil Gupta and Brian Kenny, 'Inside Amazon's Growth Strategy', *Harvard Business Review*, July 2023. Available online: https://hbr.org/podcast/2023/07/inside-amazons-growth-strategy (accessed September 2025).

3 Arpan Chaturvedi, '"Worth Zero": Founder of India's Once Biggest Startup Byju's Concedes Mistakes', Reuters, 18 October 2024. Available

online: https://www.reuters.com/world/india/worth-zero-founder-indias-once-biggest-startup-byjus-concedes-mistakes-2024-10-18 (accessed September 2025).

4 'How Zoom Won the Pandemic', Harvard Business School, 8 February 2021. Available online: https://d3.harvard.edu/platform-digit/submission/how-zoom-won-the-pandemic/ (accessed September 2025).

5 Victoria Turk, 'Zoom Took Over the World. This Is What Will Happen Next', *Wired*, 5 August 2020. Available online: https://www.wired.com/story/future-of-zoom/ (accessed September 2025).

6 Paul Vigna, 'Coinbase Fetches $85 Billion Valuation in Market Debut', *Wall Street Journal*, 14 April 2021. Available online: https://www.wsj.com/finance/currencies/coinbase-shares-surge-in-trading-debut-11618421619 (accessed September 2025).

16 The Exit Mindset

1 Harry McCracken, 'When Google Bought YouTube: The Inside Story', *Fast Company*, September 2025. Available online: https://www.fastcompany.com/91408036/youtube-google-acquisition-2006-steve-chen-eric-schmidt-ate-tv-oral-history (accessed October 2025).

2 Akshay Datt, 'The Unicorn Factory: Sanjeev Bikhchandani & Info Edge', *Founder Thesis*, 1 March 2023. Available online: https://www.founderthesis.com/p/the-unicorn-factory (accessed October 2025).

3 Tami Brehse and Kylie Kirschner, 'PayPal Mafia: Elon Musk, Peter Thiel, Reid Hoffman, and the Founders Who Defined Silicon Valley', *Business Insider*, 6 December 2024. Available online: https://www.businessinsider.com/paypal-mafia-members-elon-musk-peter-thiel-reid-hoffman-companies (accessed October 2025).

4 ET Bureau, 'Walmart Acquires Flipkart for $16 Billion in World's Largest Ecommerce Deal', *Economic Times*, 10 May 2018. Available online: https://economictimes.indiatimes.com/small-biz/startups/newsbuzz/walmart-acquires-flipkart-for-16-bn-worlds-largest-ecommerce-deal/articleshow/64095145.cms (accessed October 2025).

5 'Unveiling the Phenomenon: The Rise of the Flipkart Mafia in 2024', *Private Circle*, 15 February 2024. Available online: https://blog.privatecircle.co/unveiling-the-phenomenon-the-rise-of-the-flipkart-mafia-in-2024/ (accessed October 2025).

About the Author

Indraveer Singh is an entrepreneur, bestselling author and founder mentor with over fifteen years of experience at the intersection of startup formation, capital strategy and execution design. He has worked closely with more than 1,000 founders across edtech, SaaS, D2C, health tech and other sectors, helping them calibrate business models, structure operational systems, navigate capital decisions, and build disciplined, scalable growth pathways through his Co-Pilot Mentorship approach.

Having built and exited a global infosec venture, Indraveer Singh brings both operator depth and strategic clarity to the founder's journey. His work focuses not only on building companies but also on strengthening the founder's internal decision architecture, the core that shapes lasting ventures.

He leads 10xbox, a founder-first, retreat-driven school of entrepreneurship focused on developing entrepreneurial leadership before ventures scale. His first book, *Start It Right: A Startup Handbook*, remained an Amazon bestseller for months. His work is anchored in a clear thesis: the venture is an outcome; the founder is the cause.

Scan to connect and consult with Indraveer Singh